PLAYSCRIPT 109

THE POWER OF THE DOG

Howard Barker

JOHN CALDER : LONDON
RIVERRUN PRESS : NEW YORK

First published in Great Britain, 1985, by
John Calder (Publishers) Limited
18 Brewer Street, London W1R 4AS

and in the United States of America, 1985, by
Riverrun Press Inc
175 Fifth Avenue
New York, NY 10010

All performing rights in this play are strictly reserved and
applications for performance should be made to:

Judy Daish Associates Limited
83 Eastbourne Mews, London W2 6LQ

No performance of this play may be given unless a licence has
been obtained prior to rehearsal.

British Library Cataloguing in Publication Data
Barker, Howard
   The power of the dog: moments in history
   and anti-history.—(Play series; 109)
   I. Title
   822'.914   PR6052.A6485

ISBN 0 7145 4066 8

SUBSIDISED BY THE
Arts Council
OF GREAT BRITAIN

Typeset 9/10 pt Press Roman by Gilbert Composing Services,
   Leighton Buzzard, Bedfordshire.
Printed in Great Britain by Photobooks (Bristol) Ltd

THE POWER OF THE DOG

Moments in History and Anti-History

Characters

McGROOT	A Comedian
POSKREBYSHEV	A Secretary
STALIN	A Politician
MOLOTOV	A Politician
CHURCHILL	A Politician
ENGLISH INTERPRETER	
RUSSIAN INTERPRETER	
DIPLOMAT	
ILONA	A Photographer
VICTOR	A Photographer
ARKOV	A Russian Officer
SORGE	A Russian Officer
MATRIMOVA	A Russian Infantrywoman
NEESKIN	A Russian Infantrywoman
TREMBLAYEV	A Russian Infantrywoman
MELANKOV	A Russian Infantryman
GASSOV	A Russian Infantryman
GLORIA	An SS Officer
DONKIN	An Intellectual
ZDHANOV	An Intellectual
LASHENKO	An Official
BUBER	A Tradesman
TOSHACK	A Town Councillor
MAN IN OVERCOAT	
WAITERS	
WORKMEN	

'Deliver my soul from the sword,
My darling from the power of the dog.'

Psalm 22

The Power of the Dog was first presented at the Lyceum Studio theatre, Edinburgh, on 14th November, 1984 by The Joint Stock Theatre Company, with the following cast:

McGROOT	Matthew Scurfield
POSKREBYSHEV	Sean Baker
STALIN	Philip McGough
MOLOTOV	*
CHURCHILL	Peter Sproule
ENGLISH INTERPRETER+	Hugh Fraser
DIPLOMAT+	Hugh Fraser
RUSSIAN INTERPRETER	Amelda Brown
ILONA	Stephanie Fayerman
VICTOR	Sean Baker
ARKOV	Peter Sproule
SORGE	Hugh Fraser
MATRIMOVA	Amelda Brown
NEESKIN	Catherine McDonagh
TREMBLAYEV	Tamara Hinchco
MELANKOV	Matthew Scurfield
GASSOV	Philip McGough
GLORIA	Tamara Hinchco
DONKIN	Tamara Hinchco
ZDHANOV	Peter Sproule
LASHENKO	Matthew Scurfield
TOSHACK	Matthew Scurfield
BUBER	Peter Sproule
MAN IN OVERCOAT	Sean Baker
WAITERS	The company
WORKMEN	The company

Directed by Kenny Ireland
Designed by Roger Glossop

*The part of Molotov was omitted from this production.
+These parts were combined for the purposes of this production.

A Great Man Hallucinates

A Banqueting hall in the Kremlin. Waiters laying cloths. A clown practises juggling.

McGROOT. The mon tells me this is an honour. Wha' kind of honour, says A, A ha' spent ma life avoidin' honours—the honour o' servin' wi' His Majesty's forces, the honour o' makin' a wooman decent in the eyes o' God, the honour o' buyin' the boss a drink, cheers, but honour's somethin' A can do wi'out. He says, the honour o' bein' the furst Scotsman to appear in the Kremlin. A pretended ta think aboot it—well, ye gotta look serious, haven't ye—an' then A said, wi' all respect, A'm perfectly happy wi' the circus, A've noo great ambition to play the Kremlin, it's noo a billin' A'm so desperate for. But he's very persistent—they can be persistent, can't they —he tells me this is one honour A canna refuse, there's noo exactly a glut o' Scots entertainers in the USSR. A was put on the shortlist—in fact, A was at the top of it—in fact, there was only one name on it—an' he showed it to me, an' there it was—Archie McGroot. A looked at it a minute. Archie McGroot, ma name's Vladimir Galoshev—(STALIN *enters, with his* AIDES. McGROOT *drops the balls)*—fuck—*(he scrambles after them)* A will noo survive this . . . A will noo see the streets o' Paisley underneath ma boots agin, A'm a doomed mon—*(He drops the balls again)* Christ . . . ! *(He retrieves them)* He does noo laugh, it's like flashin' yer bollocks in the convent—*He walks on his hands to where* STALIN *is idly tasting food)* **Wha' did the Emperor say to the clown?** (STALIN *ignores him)* **Wha' did the Emperor say to the clown?** (STALIN *wanders off)* Fuckin' hell, A should ha' stayed in the clubs, but A'm an idealist . . .

MOLOTOV.   What did the Emperor say to the clown?

McGROOT *(flipping onto his feet)*. **Lend us yer trousers, Harry!**

MOLOTOV.   Lend us your trousers . . . ?

STALIN.   Does Churchill find Scotsmen funny?

POSKREBYSHEV *(reading from a list)*.   He enjoys cheese on toast, playing draughts, and a singer called George Robey. We could not find George Robey.

STALIN.   This is a Scotsman.

MOLOTOV.   Yes, but I'm afraid he isn't very funny . . .

McGROOT.   **Noo funny! Who says a'm noo funny!**

POSKREBYSHEV.   There are very few Scottish clowns in Russia.

STALIN.   I will sit here, and they will sit there.

McGROOT *(to STALIN)*.   Hullo, Jock! A luv yer whiskers!

STALIN.   Molotov will sit on my right . . .

McGROOT.   If every whisker was a kulak, how many barbers wud ye need?

POSKREBYSHEV.   The General Secretary is not enjoying your performance.

McGROOT.   He is, but he woon't admit it—A've cum across that before, A been booed offstage because they were so pleased wi' me—

STALIN.   Tell him I will kick his arse . . .

McGROOT.   Thank yoo! *(He rolls into a ball)* It is a fact that the more resistance you encounter, the more effective yoo are bein'! A take a kick in the bollocks as a positive sign o' favour, it's all part o' bein' a radical comedian—*(He wiggles towards* STALIN, *arse rampant)* Goo on, kick it, A've noo pride in tha' particular region, A doona keep ma brains there like sum people—(STALIN *goes to kick it.* McGROOT *tumbles under a table)*

MOLOTOV.   Churchill wants to thank you for Stalingrad.

POSKREBYSHEV *(with a bowl)*.   The roses have just arrived from the Caucasus! Smell that!

MOLOTOV.   He has a present for you, I warn you.

STALIN *(smelling the bowl)*.   I haven't a present for him.

MOLOTOV.   What is there to thank him for?

STALIN.   I only give presents for killing Germans.

POSKREBYSHEV *(sniffing)*.   Marvellous . . .

STALIN.   I wish I was in a better mood all the same. Does he have someone to taste his food? Tell him I understand if he wants a food taster, I will not interpret it as bad manners, though it must be obvious it is in the interests of the Soviet Union to keep him alive, his party is full of Nazi sympathizers.

McGROOT *(poking his head out from under a table)*.   There was a Socialist, an Anarchist, and a Communist, an' they all wanted a new pair o' trousers—

STALIN.   I feel miserable, why?

McGROOT.   So they went to this capitalist trouser-maker, and the Socialist said, if ye make me a pair o' trousers, A will give ye thirty roubles. Thirty roubles, says the capitalist, tha' will noo pay the wages o' ma worker, nor the cost of th' electricity, nor the rent of ma factory, let aloon ma profit, so you stuff yer thirty roubles, A will noo make ye a pair of trousers for less than a hundred—

STALIN *(sitting disconsolately)*.   Why? Is somebody against me?

McGROOT.   So the Socialist thinks for a minute, and then he goes to the bank an' he takes oot a loan, goos back to the capitalist an' gives him the hundred roubles. An' the capitalist gives him a pair o' trousers. And then the Anarchist comes along, an' he says, if ye make me a pair o' trousers, A will give ye thirty roubles. Thirty roubles, says the capitalist—

STALIN.   Somebody is . . . against me . . . . .

POSKREBYSHEV.   Not necessarily, it may be just a headache . . .

McGROOT.   Tha' will noo pay the wages o' ma worker, nor the cost o' th' electricity, nor the rent o' ma factory, let aloon ma profit, A will noo make ye a pair o' trousers for less than a hundred. So the anarchist thinks for a minute, an' then he goos to the bank, an' he robs it, an' he goes back to the capitalist, an' he pays him the hundred, an' the capitalist gives him a pair o' trousers . . . are ye still with me?

WAITER.   The English are coming!

McGROOT.   Fuck the English, A have n'a finished yet! *(The WAITERS take up their positions around the tables. POSKREBYSHEV goes to a gramophone. STALIN does not move)* So then the Communist comes along an' he says, if ye make me a pair o' trousers, A will give ye thirty roubles. Thirty roubles, say the capitalist, tha' will noo pay the wages of ma worker, nor the cost o' th' electricity, nor the rent of ma factory, let aloon ma profit! A will noo make ye a pair o' trousers for less than a hundred. So the Communist thinks for a minute, an' then he goes away an' starts a revolution to abolish trousers. *(Pause, then MOLOTOV bursts out laughing)* Ye got to tell a joke agin yersel' sometimes . . .

POSKREBSHEV *puts the needle on the record. The sound of 'Land of Hope and Glory' echoes through the Kremlin. CHURCHILL enters with a DIPLOMAT and an INTERPRETER. He stands for a few bars, quite rigid. POSKREBYSHEV lifts the needle off, abruptly. Pause.*

CHURCHILL *(to the INTERPRETER).*   Tell Generalissimo Stalin, that it brings tears to my eyes to hear the music of my country echo through the chambers of this august edifice . . .

ENG INTERPRETER.   Prime Minister Churchill wishes you to know it brings tears to his eyes to hear his country's music playing in this place . . .

STALIN.   Tell the Prime Minister it is a sign of his greatness that he cries out of love for his people. . .

SOVIET INTERPRETER.   Generalissimo Stalin says it is a sign of the Prime Minister's greatness that he—

McGROOT.   Oh, fuckin' hell, yoo compliment me and A'll compliment yoo—

CHURCHILL.   The great Soviet people, and the great English people—

McGROOT.   Never mind the Scots, they're just cunts—

CHURCHILL.   Join hands in this epic struggle—

ENG INTERPRETER.   The great Soviet people and the great English people—

McGROOT.   A do love you, Oh, A do love you!

ENG INTERPRETER.   Join hands in this epic struggle—

CHURCHILL.   I bring you from my master—

ENG INTERPRETER.   He brings you from his master—

CHURCHILL.   The great King George, by grace of God—

ENG INTERPRETER.   By grace of God—

CHURCHILL.   This weapon, forged of English steel—

ENG INTERPRETER.   A weapon made of English steel—

CHURCHILL.   The sword of Stalingrad—

ENG INTERPRETER.   The sword of Stalingrad. *(Pause)*

CHURCHILL.   Give it to me, then. *(*DIPLOMAT *removes it from a case,* *hands it to* CHURCHILL*)* Does he want it or not? *(They look at* STALIN, *who moves towards* CHURCHILL *and takes it. Then he kisses it)* Why is he crying? Don't translate that.

DIPLOMAT.   They lost three-quarters of a million men.

CHURCHILL.   No. . . it is because of the King. It is the power of monarchy . .

McGROOT.   Fuckin' hell it is . . .

CHURCHILL.   I ask Generalissimo Stalin, would he care, for my erudition, to propose a definition of History?

ENG INTERPRETER.   Mr Churchill asks Stalin, how does he define History.

MOLOTOV.   I propose a toast!

SOV INTERPRETER.   Mr Molotov requests a toast—

MOLOTOV.   To the Collective Farms!

SOV INTERPRETER.   The Collective Farms!

CHURCHILL ETC.   The Collective Farms . . .

STALIN.   History? *(He stands, leans on his table)*

CHURCHILL.   No doubt we are about to hear something of the dialectical mumbo jumbo of the communist mind . . .

STALIN.   History? *(Pause)* The incredulous overwhelmed by the incredible . . . *(Pause. He sits)*

SOV INTERPRETER.   Er. . . the unbelievable . . . er . . .

ENG INTERPRETER.   The unlikely . . . . triumphing over . . .

McGROOT *(emerging).*   History! A will tell ye wha' history is, it's a woman bein' raped by ten soldiers in a village in Manchuria . . .

CHURCHILL.   I see entertainment has been laid on, of a most succulent kind . . .

ENG INTERPRETER.   The unbelieving meeting the . . . er . . . *(He looks to the* SOVIET INTERPRETER*)* dyoksavna . . . ?

CHURCHILL.   My love of Scottish comedians has been noted, but alas, not satisfied . . . Tell Mr Molotov, I drink to the Red Army.

ENG INTERPRETER.   Mr Churchill drinks to the Red Army—

MOLOTOV.   The Red Army!

CHURCHILL.   The robust Ivan, fearless in battle and loyal in heart— translate—

ENG INTERPRETER.   The er . . . wonderful Ivan . . . er . . . unafraid . . . and . . .

McGROOT.   Wha's the difference between history and a hysterectomy? One's done wi' a scalpel and the other wi' a bayonet—

STALIN.   I drink to the appearance of the English army . . .

SOV INTERPRETER.   The General Secretary toasts the coming of the English soldiers!

STALIN.   Are the English afraid of the Germans?

CHURCHILL.   What's he say?

ENG INTERPRETER.   Er . . . he wonders if . . . er . . .

STALIN.   To fight a war, you must first get near the enemy . . .

CHURCHILL.   What's he say?

ENG INTERPRETER.   He says . . . er . . . you have to . . . he implies the

British are . . . er . . . unwilling to—

STALIN.   You cannot fight a war with banks. Tanks, yes, but not banks! *(MOLOTOV laughs)*

ENG INTERPRETER.   He says the banks are all very well, but—

McGROOT.   There was an Englishman, a Scotsman, and an Irishman, and they were all scared o' the Germans! *(STALIN laughs, applauds)* Christ! A goot somewhere! Shall A say it agin? *(He goes to a waiter)* Hey, have ye heard this?

CHURCHILL.   I have not travelled across the seas and the great land masses of this continent, tell him—

SOV INTERPRETER.   Mr Churchill has not come all this way—

CHURCHILL.   In order to submit to a calculated and unjust reprimand—

McGROOT *(doing a headstand)*.   If all politicians were liars, would anything be any different? Correction! If they all told the truth, would anything be any different?

STALIN.   I would give up all the authority I possess to meet a beautiful woman on a train . . .

McGROOT.   Like hell ye wuld . . . .

ENG INTERPRETER.   Stalin says . . .

CHURCHILL.   . . .that he cast aspersions on the honour of the English people . . . .

ENG INTERPRETER.   . . . he would give anything to meet a woman on a train . . .

STALIN.   It is a sad fact I cannot meet a woman on a train unless both the woman and the train are commandeered for me. But of course that entirely removes the significance of the occasion. Accident, which is the essence of experience, has been eliminated from my life . . .

ENG INTERPRETER.   He says, such opportunities don't . . . come his way that often . . . .

STALIN.   Has Churchill ever met a beautiful woman on a train?

ENG INTERPRETER.   He asks—the connotations are humorous—if you, Churchill, have encountered a lady in a railway compartment—

CHURCHILL.   I have met my wife.

SOV INTERPRETER.   Churchill says he has met Mrs Churchill— *(MOLOTOV bursts out laughing)*

CHURCHILL.   What is so amusing about my wife?

McGOOT.   In Manchester a geezer is lookin' at a woman in a train. In Manchuria they are cuttin' a woman's breasts off wi' a bayonet, ye gotta laugh, noo, ye gotta laugh!

MOLOTOV.   I propose a toast—

SOV INTERPRETER.   Molotov toasts—

MOLOTOV.   Mrs Churchill!

CHURCHILL ETC.   My wife.

McGROOT.   The woman in Manchester says to the woman in Manchuria, this geezer keeps starin' at me, wha' shall A do?

CHURCHILL.   Tell Stalin, if he wants to meet women in trains he should be a clerk—

McGROOT.   So the woman from Manchuria says, ye call tha' a problem, A got ten soldiers here are gonna murder me! Ooh, says the woman from

Manchester, but they're beasts, a'nt they? **Noo funny! Tha's noo funny! Tha' is a fuckin' disgrace!**

CHURCHILL.   The great man endures his loneliness with few compensations but the certain knowledge of his immortality . . .

ENG INTERPRETER.   Er. . . . it's . . . a lonely life in politics . . .

MOLOTOV *(taking a glass)*.   To the Red October tractor plant!

ENG INTERPRETER.   Red October Tractor Plant . . .

CHURCHILL.   I wonder if we should not move to the question of the future of the European people's. Translate . . .

ENG INTERPRETER.   Mr Churchill would like to talk about . . . the post-war settlement . . .

CHURCHILL.   The British government cannot concede that the social systems of the countries liberated from the heel of Nazidom shall be dictated by the colour of troops who stand upon their soil . . .

MOLOTOV.   Especially since the English soldiers persist in standing on their own soil. Well, it is a very understandable point of view . . . .

ENG INTERPRETER.   Molotov says . . . observes . . .

CHURCHILL.   What does Stalin say? I do not listen to the puppet, only the puppet master. *(*STALIN *is fixed, absent)*

McGROOT.   Wha' is it, Joe? Cum on, son . . .

MOLOTOV *(Raising his glass)*.   The Black Sea torpedo boats!

ENG INTERPRETER *(standing, shakily)*.   The Black Sea . . . Christ . . .

MOLOTOV ETC.   The Black Sea torpedo boats!

McGROOT.   There was a great mun, an' he chopped half the people's heads off to make the other half better, an' when he got to the pearly gates, he said to God, didn' A do well, A only killed half the people, an' God said, yoo are a merciless bastard, an' A will put yoo in hell. An' then another great mun arrived at the pearly gates, an' he didna chop anyone's head off, but he never made 'em better either, an' he said to God, didn' A do well, A never killed noobody, an' God said, yoo are a complacent bastard, an' A will put yoo in hell too. An' the two great men looked at one another in the flamin' furnace, an' said, wha' the fuck does God want, then? And there came a terrible roar out o' Heaven an' a voice said—CHARITY. *(Pause)* do ye get that'? A doon't . . .

STALIN.   What does Churchill want to see in Greece . . . ?

ENG INTERPRETER.   He asks what you would like in Greece.

CHURCHILL.   Tell him I should like, if there is a monarch available, to instal him there . . .

CHURCHILL.   The kingdom of the Hellenes would delight me profoundly—

STALIN.   He can have Greece, but not Bulgaria—

ENG INTERPRETER.   Greece is okay, but we can't have Bulgaria—

CHURCHILL.   What about Italy?

ENG INTERPRETER.   Italy?

STALIN.   I do not care for Italy.

ENG INTERPRETER.   Italy's all right—

CHURCHILL.   A Polish king would be a nice thing, too—

SOV INTERPRETER.   What about a monarchy in Poland?

MOLOTOV.   There are two million dead Russians in Poland!
CHURCHILL.   I cannot see the objection to a monarchy . . .
MOLOTOV.   We will have preponderance in Poland.
CHURCHILL.   Who's got a bit of paper?
ENG INTERPRETER.   I've got an envelope . . . .
DIPLOMAT.   What about Roumania?
MOLOTOV.   Fifty per cent.
SOV INTERPRETER.   Fifty per cent . . .
DIPLOMAT *(scrawling).*   Hang on . . . Bulgaria, no . . . .
CHURCHILL.   Italy, put Italy . . .

As they huddle over the paper, STALIN *rises suddenly to his feet.*

STALIN.   What is that man doing?
POSKREBYSHEV.   Where?
STALIN.   That man!
POSKREBYSHEV.   He is a waiter.
STALIN.   He is rubbing my face with a pencil . . . .
POSKREBYSHEV.   Sorry . . . ?
STALIN.   **A waiter you call him!** *(*MOLOTOV *looks round. The* WAITER
   is aghast)   Why is he rubbing my face with a pencil? If he's a waiter? Go
   on, explain that.
POSKREBYSHEV.   Er . . .
STALIN.   If he's a simple, common or garden waiter, why is he rubbing me
   out?
MOLOTOV.   Rubbing you—
STALIN.   **Yes!**
POSKREBYSHEV.   Could you—expand on what—
STALIN.   **I don't have to expand anything, it's obvious what's going on!**
POSKREBYSHEV.   Yes—
STALIN.   **Stop it, then.** *(Pause)*
POSKREBYSHEV.   Yes . . .

POSKREBYSHEV *goes to the* WAITER, *whispers to him, and the man starts
to leave.*

STALIN.   He has scissors in his hand.
POSKREBYSHEV.   Scissors?
STALIN.   **Do I have to repeat myself? It's scissors he's got!** *(*CHURCHILL
   and his AIDES *look up)* For cutting me out of the films . . . the man with
   the miniature paintbrush is turning my face into sky . . . a lifetime's work,
   painting Stalin out of every frame . . . one idle moment, dreaming of cunt
   in the archives, and I slip by—there, I saw him, behind Lenin, don't blink!
   It was Stalin!
MOLOTOV.   Ask him if he's tired . . .
POSKREBYSHEV.   You ask him.
STALIN.   **I don't trust one of you! There is the only one I can trust!** *He
   indicates* CHURCHILL) Because he is my enemy . . .

CHURCHILL. What's he saying?

ENG INTERPRETER. It's Georgian . . . . dialect stuff . . .

CHURCHILL. Is it bawdy?

ENG. INTERPRETER. I think it is, yes . . .

STALIN. My picture has been reproduced more than any man's . . . when the wind blows I drift down in gardens and parks . . .

POSKREBYSHEV. Yes . . .

STALIN. . . . the waiters are planning to wipe me away . . .

POSKREBYSHEV. I don't think—

STALIN. Shh! Millions of waiters will go around Moscow, removing my face from the walls. Waiters are like that. It's time for a purge.

POSKREBYSHEV. Yes.

STALIN. Ask Churchill, what will they do to him when he's dead?

SOV INTERPRETER. Stalin asks, what will they do to Churchill when he is dead.

CHURCHILL. Honour me.

STALIN. There are no mirrors to Stalin. Only his portrait sycophantically done . . . *(he turns)* **Who will know me when I'm dead!**

POSKREBYSHEV. Me . . ?

CHURCHILL. Tell Stalin there is nothing like the truth. It is the steel that cuts the Gordian knot of autocracy . . .

ENG INTERPRETER. Er . . .

CHURCHILL. Translate it . . .

ENG INTERPRETER. Churchill says there is nothing like the truth . . . when it comes to . . .

STALIN. Tell Churchill he can go now . . .

CHURCHILL. Honour and truth are the twin gryphons of proper authority . . .

ENG INTERPRETER. Oh, fuck . . .

CHURCHILL. Bearing in their horny claws the shield of munificience . . .

ENG INTERPRETER. I really cannot . . . translate this fucking . . .

CHURCHILL. It is the eagle swooping from the clouds of darkness . . .

ENG INTERPRETER. Stuff . . .

POSKREBYSHEV. Stalin has finished talking. *(Pause.* CHURCHILL *etc stand unsteadily)*

CHURCHILL. Is it not an awesome power, ask him, that no-one in this continent, no child nor woman, shall live without our caveat?

DIPLOMAT. He doesn't mean caveat . . . he means . . .

CHURCHILL. No medieval prince, howsoever unrestrained, could reach down as we do—

DIPLOMAT. Not caveat—surely—

CHURCHILL. —into the lives of the as yet unborn, and stir their entrails . . . history . . . history . . . hold my hand . . . hold my hand . . . *(He extends it in a drunken passion to* STALIN, *who does not reciprocate)* **Is anybody translating this?** *(People are drifting away)*

MOLOTOV. Good night! Good night!

CHURCHILL *(withdrawing his hand).* Good night, you foul genius . . . Good night . . .

The English go out. The WAITERS *stand by the tables.* MOLOTOV *pours himself a drink.*

STALIN *(at last).*   Somewhere in the Polish desert is a little photographer. Bring him to Stalin. *(Pause.* POSKREBYSHEV *looks to* MOLOTOV)
POSKREBYSHEV *(taking out his notebook).*   You wouldn't happen to know the name . . .
STALIN.   No, I don't know the name . . .
POSKREBYSHEV.   We will round up all the photographers. Did you say little?
STALIN.   Littler than Stalin.
POSKREBYSHEV.   What . . . under five feet? *(Pause)* Five-feet-six inches? *(*STALIN *just stares at the* WAITERS, *who, on a signal from* MOLOTOV, *have started clearing the tables)* Five-feet-six . . . *(He writes it down)*
STALIN.   We must wipe out the waiters . . . *(The* WAITERS *stiffen)*
POSKREBYSHEV.   What . . . in the restaurants . . .
STALIN.   Not in the fucking restaurants. Do you take me for an idiot? He thinks I am an idiot. He thinks I am intuitive—
POSKREBYSHEV.   No, I—
STALIN *(to* MOLOTOV*).*   Who are they?
MOLOTOV.   They are lieutenants in the NKVD.
STALIN.   Quite . . . *(Pause)*
POSKREBYSHEV.   Ah . . .
STALIN.   He understands . . . *(*McGROOT *appears from under a tablecloth)*
McGROOT.   Is it okay if A goo now? *(No one replies)* Where shall A collect ma fee from? Is it the geezer doon the corridor or . . . *(silence)* A'll see masel' oot . . . *(he starts to leave, stops)* The gag aboot the women, A meant to say . . . *(Pause. He turns to go.* STALIN *suddenly bursts out laughing)* Wha' did A say? *(and laughs)* Noo, noo, hang aboot, wha' did A say? A'll say it agin, shall A? *(He walks backwards)* Where was A? *(The lights fade)* McGroot's the name, Archie McGroot—*(*STALIN *laughs again)* Fuck me, A'm doin' well all of a sudden—*(it is black)* Noo, noo, ye're overdoin' it, yoo are, yoo make me feel embarassed . . . . thank yoo . . . . thank yoo . . .

The Banality of Yet Another Murder

Somewhere in the Polish Plain. A DEAD WOMAN *is hanging from a rope. A* YOUNG WOMAN, *chic but dirty, stands underneath. A* PHOTO-GRAPHER *underneath a cloth adjusts a tripod camera. The* WOMAN *strikes a pose.*

ILONA.   Her stockings are quite clean. Why did she put clean stockings on? And brush her shoes? She did, look . . . Are you ready? I look up, I— *(she breaks the pose)* Would you object if I removed the stockings? No, not for the photograph, silly. I will do, if you don't mind. *(She strikes the pose again)* I interpret silence as approval. *(A protest from under the cloth)* You took a wallet! Yes, you did! You took a snakeskin wallet from the dying officer! *(She poses)* I look up, I—*(a protest)* What is wrong with my expression! *(Muffled voice)* No I wouldn't touch her underwear! Silk notwithstanding I—*(she lifts the dead woman's skirt quickly)* Anyway, it's not, so—*(she poses)* I look up, I—*(a protest)* **This is my human condition face.** *(Murmurs)* You say it's stockings, I say it's human condition— *(protests)* Yes, I know you are looking through the lens and I am not— *(protests)* **It is not stockings it is lachrymae rerum, all right?** It is— Weltschmertz . . . *(moans)* All right, I will—

She abandons her pose and begins unhitching the woman's stockings. The PHOTOGRAPHER *appears from under the cloth.*

VICTOR.   There is the photograph I ought to take . . .

ILONA.   Who's stopping you?

VICTOR.   The dead thighs robbed. The knees offended.

IONA *(stuffing the stockings in her pocket)*.   Do you want to carry on? There is a perfect sky. *(Pause)*

VICTOR.   You haven't put her shoes on . . .

ILONA.   Never mind, she says . . . *(ignoring her, he retrieves the shoes)* Shall I tell you what I believe? I believe that every murder is an acquiescence, and every victim possessed the means of her escape. I believe in your eyes and in your mouth you own the means of your salvation, whether you want to be loved, or whether you want to be saved. At the door of the restaurant, or the gate of the camp . . . *(Pause)* She thought so, too, which is why she put her best things on . . .

VICTOR *(throwing down the shoes)*.   **They won't go on . . . !**

ILONA.   You walk through History . . . in polished shoes . . . you dance on tanks . . . you don't refuse . . . and if you die . . . you may not feel it . . . arbitrary, you can't conceal it . . . but only if the shot comes from the back . . . if you can catch his eye . . . you're all right, Jack . . . *(she takes out a map and studies it)*

VICTOR.   I wish I was a camera . . . I would have no feelings . . . my shutter wouldn't jam with shock . . . like eyelids which shut tight and lock . . . my lens would stay all hard and glassy . . . *(ILONA stands up suddenly)* If I was staring at a ditch of murder . . .

ILONA.   Shut up . . .

VICTOR.   Or a tart whose tits were classy . . .

ILONA.   **Shut up.** *(She goes to the hanged woman, stares at her)* I think that is my sister . . . *(A* RUSSIAN OFFICER *enters)*

ARKOV.   The German is not a beast.

The German is not a beast.

The German is not a beast. *(Pause)*

Human nature is not fixed but fluid, is not a granite monolith but a blank sheet of paper on which is written the social and political conjunction of its time. Man is neither good nor bad but an infinity of possibility waiting to be chosen. Have you certification entitling you to photograph in a combat zone? *(They are silent)* My brother died in Byelorussia, my mother was murdered in Kerch. But we do not talk of private losses. How can you reconstruct if you are undermined by grief? Everyone has lost and who would benefit from competition in suffering? All right, you can go. *(VICTOR makes to move)* Did you show me your certification? *(Pause)*

ILONA *(quickly)*.   Yes. *(They move swiftly to go)*

ARKOV.   You must think I am silly. I am letting you go because you are a woman.

ILONA.   Yes . . .

ARKOV.   I must say that while objectively I am unable to regard the German as a beast, I do abhor the fact he kills so many women.

ILONA.   Yes . . .

ARKOV.   Not that my regret is of the slightest significance in the scales of History.

ILONA.   No, indeed . . . *(She signals VICTOR to pack up more quickly. They start to go)*

ARKOV.   I mean, women are love. *(Pause)* Not that love is of the slightest significance, either. I regret it all the same. Will you take my photograph and never mind the combat zone certificate? *(VICTOR nods agreement)* May I stand close to you as if to indicate we are acquainted, if not intimately, then at least—

ILONA.   **That is my sister on the rope.**

ARKOV.   I do understand that. I do not mind a smile which is thoroughly enigmatic . . . *(he poses, close to her)*

ILONA.   Quick . . . .

ARKOV *(as VICTOR sets up)*.   That is an ancient camera. I have a Leica with apertures from 1 to 22.

ILONA.   It was my father's.

ARKOV.   Is that so?

ILONA.   He carted it through Europe on his back.

ARKOV.   Ah.

ILONA.   In the last war. In the last slaughter. From Lemberg to Caporetto—

ARKOV.   You are not smiling . . . .

ILONA.   From the Isonzo to the Prut—

ARKOV.   But never mind . . .

ILONA.   He left five hundred plates of dying Austrians. His best were scenes in dressing stations. Later on, he specialized in bowls of fruit— *(VICTOR takes the photograph)* **Who is going to bury my sister. . . .**

A MAN enters in a long overcoat. He walks to the hanged woman and takes her gently by the ankles.

SORGE.   This is a wonderful century. *(Pause. he looks at them)* I hold her ankles and I say **this is a wonderful century . . . .**

The Soldiers Fictionalize Their History

Shouting SOLDIERS.

MATRIMOVA. The student Georgina Matrimova of the School of Film and Poetry of the University of Sverdlovsk, temporarily attached to the Support Unit of the 72nd Motorized Division, presents her innovatory Celluloid-Free film entitled WAR . . . ! *(The* SOLIDERS *punctuate her statement with a roar of battle)* In this celluloid-free film the battle sequences achieve a degree of realism never before encountered in the history of the cinema! *(They roar)* Unflinching detail of a night attack against the Fascist lines renders all previous examples of the genre artificial and redundant. **Roll!**

The lights go out. In the darkness the actors simulate a battle of great ferocity. They stop dead when the lights come on. One of them walks forward holding his boots.

MELANKOV. The Story of the Boots. *(The rest groan)* If only these boots could talk, what a story they would tell . . .
MATRIMOVA. Close up boots . . . !
MELANKOV *(mechanically)*. Because these are not ordinary boots, these are not—*(he dries)* Shit . . .
MATRIMOVA *(prompting)*. Covet . . . .
MELANKOV. Sorry?
MATRIMOVA. Covet . . .
MELANKOV. Thou shalt not covet thy comrade's boots . . .
MATRIMOVA. Stock film of Soviet infantry!
MELANKOV *(marching on the spot)*. Private Shishkin was not born to die in socks . . .
MATRIMOVA. Zoom feet!
MELANKAKOV. His mum and dad will never know how Private Shishkin's comrades longed for him to stop a shot . . .
ALL. **Bang!**
GASSOV *(running forward)*. The Hungry Soldiers Find a Pig.
MATRIMOVA. Sound effect!
NEESKIN *(narrating)*. Owing to the speed of our advance the kitchens have been—
MATRIMOVA. **Sound effect!** *(The* SOLDIERS *squeal)*
MELANKOV. Georgina, you have cut my line about the—
NEESKIN. The kitchens are fully fifty kilometres in the rear!
MATRIMOVA. Stock film of tanks!
MELANKOV *(still holding the boots)*. Thank you, cunt . . .
GASSOV. Is it a mirage, or is it a pig?
MELANKOV. Any time you want the boots, tell me and I'll just—
ALL. **It's a pig!**
MELANKOV. say fuck off—
MATRIMOVA. Comic sequence of animal evading capture! *(A tumbling*

of SOLDIERS*)* And cut to face of outraged NCO—

GASSOV. **'O said you could fall out you!**

ALL *(acting satisfaction).* Munch, munch, munch . . .

TREMBLAYEV *(stepping forward).* A Girl Makes Love. *(Boos and groans)*

MATRIMOVA. Shh!

TREMBLAYEV. A Girl Makes Love.

MATRIMOVA. Close up Startled Peasant.

TREMBLAYEV. Language is no barrier. In war the simplest communication will suffice . . .

MATRIMOVA. Close up eyes . . .

TREMBLAYEV. He is shy and so is she . . . .

MELANKOV. Bollocks . . . .

MATRIMOVA. Sound effect of wind in trees . . . .

They susurrate. TREMBLAYEV *slowly unbuttons her tunic,* ARKOV *goes towards her. Suddenly, as he goes to touch her, she shrieks.*

TREMBLAYEV. **Not to touch me!**

MATRIMOVA. Cut! *(Jeers and boos)*

TREMBLAYEV. **I said not to touch me didn't I?**

MATRIMOVA. **Cut!**

TREMBLAYEV. You promised me he wouldn't and he—

MATRIMOVA *(distraught).* CUT! CUT!

SORGE, *still in his overcoat, walks forward from where he has witnessed the exercise.*

SORGE. The war film which merely dispenses pity does not help anyone. The experience of war is very narrow—hence the proliferation of cliches. The proper war film asks, did the soldiers die for something, or did they die for nothing? It is a revolutionary question. So the proper war film is not actually about the battle, it is about the reasons for the battle. What are the reasons for the battle? Arkov?

ARKOV *(getting up).* It's eleven o'clock and I want to write a letter.

SORGE. You write too many letters.

ARKOV. Yes, it's what I'm good at.

TREMBLAYEV. Answer the question.

ARKOV. Must I?

TREMBLAYEV. You must participate in group discussions!

ARKOV. I do participate in group discussions.

SORGE. No. You are present at group discussions. You don't participate in them. *(Pause)*

ARKOV. What was the question?

MATRIMOVA. What are the reasons for the battle? *(Pause)*

ARKOV *(routinely).* The liberation of the homeland.

TREMBLAYEV. No!

ARKOV. Oh, Sonya, please . . .

TREMBLAYEV. The liberation of the homeland is not sufficient reason for the battle!

ARKOV *(shrugs, gets up to go)*. It's good enough for me.

TREMBLAYEV. Liberation for whom? That is the question, surely? Liberate for landlords, or liberate for peasants? Examine liberators closely!

ARKOV *(going to her)*. You have lovely tits, but you bore me to the marrow of my balls . . . *(Laughter as he goes out)*

TREMBLAYEV *(turning on GASSOV)*. What's funny about that! You don't really think that's funny, do you? *(She looks to NEESKIN)* Do you think that's funny? I don't, I think it's absolutely pitiful—

MELANKOV *(leaping out)*. **I kill the Germans! I kill the Germans!**

TREMBLAYEV *(to SORGE)*. Can we have that censured, please?

MELANKOV. **I creep to the rim of the machine gun pit!**

TREMBLAYEV. Can we?

SORGE. Yes.

MELANKOV. **The night is black and so am I . . .**

MATRIMOVA. Sorge, one day I will make a film, and it will tell the entire truth. It will contain every political truth and every personal truth. It will contain the whole of reality. I will call it WHOLEFILM. I hate partiality, I hate bits!

MELANKOV. **I wait . . . in less than thirty seconds they will be dead . . . under the stars they snore their final sleep . . . !**

SORGE. It is easy to satirize the bourgeois film but difficult to cut free from its principles. For example, the principle of courage—

MELANKOV *(clutching his face in horror)*. **Aaagghh! I, a boy from Uzbekistan who drove a tractor I will kill four Germans sleeping, aaagghh!**

MATRIMOVA. I do not like the principle of courage.

SCORGE. I think it is the principle of individual courage that you do not like.

MATRIMOVA. Yes.

SORGE.Courage in whole peoples you do like.

MATRIMOVA. Yes.

SORGE. So we must represent artistically a new form of courage, mustn't we?

MELANKOV. **I hop! I hop! I have no legs I am so springlike and so coiled! I spring! and I am in the pit and they are sleeping, they are sleeping, oh, they did not think and they are sleeping!** *(He leaps)*

SORGE. And this courage will not consist of sacrifice but will celebrate survival.

MATRIMOVA. Yes.

SORGE. It will be the opposite to bourgeois courage.

MATRIMOVA. Yes.

MELANKOV. **I stab them in their throats, I stab them in their throats, their throats! one, quick! and then! and then! quick, quick, oh, quick!**

SORGE. Not heroics, but endurance. Not bravery, but cunning.

MELANKOV. **And run! run! my back is big, is such a big back bounding through the night, don't shoot me, I am only seventeen!**

MATRIMOVA. Thank you. You see, I am only satirical because I have such a longing to be—incredibly serious.

SORGE. Yes.

MELANKOV. **And down! down in the soft, safe earth, my love, my dearest, oh, my fucking love, I stuff the snow into my gob and taste, and taste! I live! you see, I live and they don't!** *(Pause)* They don't . . . they don't . . . they don't . . . . *(Pause)*

SORGE. Don't let me keep you up . . . *(The soldiers wander off, except TREMBLAYEV)* Did you want something? *(He looks at her. Pause)*

TREMBLAYEV. I can't sleep because of you. *(Pause. He wanders a little)* Did you hear me?

SORGE. Yes.

TREMBLAYEV. It is not worth going to bed because all I do is think of you—

SORGE. Comrade—

TREMBLAYEV. Sighing and so on, turning over all the time I keep the other women up, I—

SORGE. Listen, Comrade—

TREMBLAYEV. Please don't patronize me, will you! *(Pause)* I was a secretary before the war. Earrings, nail varnish, giving the eye in corridors and rotting my bras with desperate little sweats, I wouldn't care if I was killed tomorrow, I have lived more in the last two years than all my—

SORGE. I wonder if you shouldn't—

TREMBLAYEV. **I haven't finished yet.** *(Pause)* You cannot just do this to me—alter my life—drain me, wash me out and fill me up again when—

SORGE. What?

TREMBLAYEV. **I think you have a responsibility.** *(Pause)* You deliberately set out to undermine my personality—you did—to demolish everything I was—for which I am entirely grateful—and to exert a power over my emotions which—

SORGE. Comrade, I am going to recommend you take special leave—

TREMBLAYEV. YOU DID, YOU KNOW YOU DID, WHY ARE YOU SUCH A LIAR?

SORGE. It is my primary function as political officer with this regiment to carry out instruction—

TREMBLAYEV. Shut up.

SORGE. In the materialist conception of history and the—

TREMBLAYEV. Shut up or I will slap your face. *(He turns to go)* I am fucking with Roy, have you noticed? *(He goes out)* LIAR, YOU HAVE! *(ILONA enters)*

ILONA. Someone has pinched my sister's body. Where is it, please? *(TREMBLAYEV looks at her)* They put her under a tarpaulin. Now she's gone. So has the tarpaulin.

TREMBLAYEV. I am not responsible for bodies. I am a rocket instructor. *(She goes out. GASSOV passes. She accosts him)*

ILONA. Have you seen it?

GASSOV. What?

ILONA. The body.

GASSOV. Which body? I have been in action continuously since Stalingrad. Which body do you mean?

ILONA.   I have a sister. Her name is Hannela. I found her hanging over there. They took her down. They covered her in a tarpaulin. Now she's gone. So has the tarpaulin.

GASSOV.   I expect they put her in a hole.

ILONA.   On whose authority?

GASSOV.   It's not a question of authority. It's an instinct.

ILONA.   She's been stolen.

GASSOV.   It is one of the major achievements of the Red Army to have disposed efficiently of 20 million murdered people. Some say a hundred million. I don't know. But that is a lot of holes. And the tanks go very quickly, leaving fields of dead behind . . .

ILONA.   I have been robbed.

GASSOV *(as* VICTOR *enters).*   Sometimes they dig up bits from other wars. In Prezymsl, under all the shattered concrete, they found a Teutonic knight still upright on his horse. I didn't see it. And a Swedish pikeman whose blue eyes were pickled in a bog. But the sanitary squads are obsessive liars, perhaps because the work was boring. Are you sure you had a sister? (ILONA *stares in disbelief*) I only ask because there are so many people claiming they're bereaved. Some invent whole families and go around in mourning. My mother starved to death in Leningrad. Now, that is true, but I haven't got the papers proving it. And that's another thing, you can't claim pension unless you have the documents. The party is aware of the tendency to fabricate dead siblings, and—

ILONA.   **I had a sister!** *(Pause)*

GASSOV.   Yes. *(He goes out.* ILONA *looks at* VICTOR*)*

ILONA.   Not that I knew her. I think of all the people I have know—and God knows I have known some—I knew her least. When I was dangling from the other tit from birth you'd think I'd know her, wouldn't you, you would think so, but I don't believe in intimacy, it tells you nothing, does it, I have never actually been close to anyone, she was more beautiful than me, **I don't understand how she got herself hanged.** *(Pause)*

VICTOR.   I don't want to change the subject, only—*(she looks at him)* Do you mind if I change the subject? I have this feeling—do you mind this—I think we're going to be shot.

ILONA.   Why?

VICTOR.   I think we've run out of luck.

ILONA.   We never had any luck.

VICTOR.   I know that, only—

ILONA.   We never wanted luck, or asked for luck, or even entertained the possibility of luck. I hate luck—it's what hope shits in a panic—

VICTOR.   Yes—

ILONA.   If we'd relied on luck we wouldn't have 18 boxes of historic photographs—

VICTOR.   Of course, I'm only saying—what am I saying—I am saying we have the most comprehensive collection of documentary suffering in the history of photography. We have hanged and murdered people from the Adriatic to the Barents Sea, which is marvellous, which is—excellent— but it is also a terrible responsibility and I—I want to go to America. *(Pause)*

ILONA. We used to go dancing together. She went to fall in love. I went to be educated. *(VICTOR puts his hands in his pockets)* I used to tell myself the education I shall get in the dance hall will be greater than the assembled libraries of the world. Of all the howling deserts of philosophy, none will teach me so much as a strange man's kiss. So I go in and wait, angling myself favourably to the floor. You may have noticed I have not got very perfect legs . . .

VICTOR *(routinely)*. No. . .

ILONA. You haven't? And I wait until I see a man who wants to kiss me—

VICTOR. With or without perfect legs—

ILONA. And there are hundreds!

VICTOR *(pacing)*. I do not want to disappear, I earned my biography so dear, sometimes to get a picture I have sweated blood, don't let some bastard with a rifle push my mouth into the mud . . .

ILONA. But eventually one shows more persistence than the others. Because he shows persistence doesn't make him the best man. It is quite possible I shall learn more from the man who is not persistent. But how can I persuade him to be competitive? It's impossible! So I end up with the persistent one.

VICTOR. I have a route worked out. It goes through Ankara and Kabul.

ILONA. And we go to a room. Not my room. His room. You cannot be educated in your own room. And we undress. And when we undress I begin to feel sad. Well, education is sad, obviously! And while his mouth is searching me I think—this was not the man. I have the wrong man again.

VICTOR. The advantage of this route is that it runs contrary to the flow of refugees.

ILONA. And I open my eyes. They hate you to open your eyes, but I cannot keep them shut, they will watch what is happening, they will witness it! My strange posture . . . my dear clothes on the bed—

VICTOR. **I have this feeling I will end up in a ditch!**

ILONA. They shout, and then—*(Pause)* that silence, oh, that lake of silence no words can cross! *(Pause)* He shuts the door, and I am in the snowy street, the wonderful snowy street, under the cold and happy stars, and on the tram which rocks me, lovingly takes my buttocks in its gentle seat . . . and I am educated, in the beauty of the ordinary, lifeless thing . . . *(VICTOR turns to go)* You are not going to America, Victor. You are sticking with this squirming old, dirty old, European place. We will find my sister, and ask her how she died. Now go to bed. *(He goes out)* To anyone who thinks it is a mystery, how we cope with so much history, I say the answer lies in pain, what my mother went through I can again. Swallow the monster and don't strain, murders from the Bosphorous to the Hebrides render all complaints absurdities. Don't ask what makes the system, if it is a system, work, cover your indignation with your foot, don't think that black stuff is burned bodies, really it is only soot . . .

Blackout.

The Limitless Absurdity of Another's Love

A room in the Kremlin. STALIN *is asleep on a couch.* PROSKEBYSHEV
enters, looks, listens, hovers, is about to steal out.

STALIN.   I'm not dead, I'm only pretending . . . . *(POSKREBYSHEV
stops)* **I'm not dead, I'm only pretending!**
POSKREBYSHEV.   I thought—he is still sleeping—I thought—
STALIN.   **Am I?**
POSKREBYSHEV *(confused).*   Are you . . . ?
STALIN.   **Dead yet?** *(Pause)*
POSKREBYSHEV.   No . . . no, you were only pretending . . . *(STALIN
sinks back with relief)*
STALIN.   I mustn't die, Poskrebyshev.
POSKREBYSHEV.   No.
STALIN.   History will never forgive me for dying at this point.
POSKREBYSHEV.   Indeed not.
STALIN.   Watch me more closely. Come in every two minutes instead of
every five.
POSKREBYSHEV.   Very well. *(He turns to go)*
STALIN.   If I appear to be in difficulties, what do you do?
POSKREBYSHEV.   I am to press the red button—
STALIN.   **No!**
POSKREBYSHEV.   No—
STALIN.   **You stupid bastard no—**
POSKREBYSHEV.   I remember, I remember—
STALIN.   **You are a—**
POSKREBYSHEV.   I know I am, I know I am—
STALIN.   What, then?
POSKREBYSHEV.   I am to shoulder the tommy-gun.
STALIN.   No doctor enters here unless covered by the tommy-gun.
POSKREBYSHEV.   I was thinking I would press the button and then
shoulder the—
STALIN.   **No!**
POSKREBYSHEV.   No, of course not—
STALIN.   **Of course not! Why not!**
POSKREBYSHEV.   Because in the panic I might forget—
STALIN.   **Yes!**
POSKREBYSHEV.   Then the doctor won't be covered and—
STALIN.   **Yes!**
POSKREBYSHEV *(counting on his fingers).*   Tommy-gun, button, guard-
alert, door—
STALIN.   And if the bastard acts suspiciously—
POSKREBYSHEV.   Shoot— —
STALIN.   There will be another one outside.
POSKREBYSHEV.   Of course. *(Pause)*
STALIN.   I am not afraid of death. I only want to postpone it as long as

possible. Don't laugh. It isn't the same thing.

POSKREBYSHEV. I wasn't laughing—

STALIN. I am bound to die eventually—

POSKREBYSHEV. Oh, I don't know—

STALIN. **Of course I will die eventually!**

POSKREBYSHEV. Eventually, I suppose—

STALIN. But when? There must come a proper moment, a moment when history will say, it was right that Stalin ceased to exercise the dictatorship of the proletariat then, but when? The problems seem to get worse, not better. Imagine if I died now, it would be a disaster! I have four hundred divisions on the Oder, this is a crucial moment in the history of the world!

POSKREBYSHEV. Absolutely. On the other hand, you are a Georgian.

STALIN. That's balls.

POSKREBYSHEV. Is it? But we have publicized the graphs of longevity in the Baku district!

STALIN. It's balls, I said. I arranged the publicity to dampen the enthusiasm of anyone anticipating my early death. There are no more centenarians in Baku than Berlin. *(The slightest pause)*

POSKREBYSHEV. Brilliant!

STALIN. There are only two classes of person able to be unreservedly themselves, to follow the absolute dictation of their personality. The supremely powerful and the utterly insane. It is the power of Marxism–Leninism that prevents me sliding from one to the other. *(*POSKREBYSHEV *turns to go)* Do I have an aura, Poskrebyshev?

POSKREBYSHEV. An aura?

STALIN. I believe the man who has emptied the cupboard of his personality creates around himself a powerful magnetic field. Do you see it?

POSKREBYSHEV. Er . . .

STALIN. Well, look, then!

POSKREBYSHEV. It isn't so much a question of actually seeing—yes, I can see it! I can see it, yes.

STALIN. What does it look like?

POSKREBYSHEV. It's—

STALIN. What? *(Pause)*

POSKREBYSHEV. I can't see it. *(He lifts his hands apologetically)* I can't actually see it, Comrade Stalin. *(Pause)*

STALIN. All right. We will find a phenomenologist. Let him investigate it.

The Poet Can Be Trusted to Castrate Himself

A table and chair. SORGE *is holding* ILONA'S *photographic plates up to the light.*

ARKOV.   You are not to censor my letters.

SORGE.   There is too much death in them. Write more about victory and less about death.

ARKOV.   I am not interested in victory.

SORGE.   That is a most peculiar sentiment for an officer of a storm battalion.

ARKOV.   Make a note of it.

SORGE.   Well, I shall, only I was thinking more of your wife. She will think you are morbid.

ARKOV.   She knows all about my morbidity.

SORGE.   She will fret. She will think you have had a premonition of your death. She will upset her neighbours on the factory bench. So the factory will produce less, and the army will be ill-equipped. The war will last longer and there will be more deaths. So you see, you contribute to the very thing that gives you most pain.

ARKOV.   I detest your facile reasoning.

SORGE.   You detest reason altogether. *(He shuts the box of plates)* Put your death interest in some poems. The letter, you see, has too much authority, the poem none at all. Later, the poem will have the authority and the letter none at all, but by then it won't matter. Do it that way, will you? I let all poems through.

ARKOV.   How would you know a poem from a letter?

SORGE.   They rhyme, don't they?

ARKOV.   You must pretend you are a philistine.

SORGE.   It shortens interviews.

ARKOV.   You are in terror of your sensitivity. You are in terror of your soul. *(He leans on the table, secretively)* One day your soul will burst out of its servitude. What then?

SORGE.   It's gone eleven o'clock . . . .

ARKOV.   And run screaming through the empty galleries of your mind. It will send the doors of your conscience flying back on their hinges, your brain will shudder with the sound of crashing doors, I pity you, you will have no sleep . . .

SORGE.   All right . . . .

ARKOV.   **I will not leave until you promise not to cut my letters up.** *(Pause)*

SORGE.   Very well, I promise.

ARKOV.   **You only promise because promises mean nothing to you!**

SORGE.   Really, Lev, you are impossible to please . . .

ILONA *(entering).*   Have I come too soon?

ARKOV.   Everything he says—everything—is utterly untrue—

SORGE.   Captain Arkov is leaving . . .

ARKOV.   Things are relatively true or relatively false—but nothing is absolutely true and nothing is absolutely false—**what are you to do with a mind like that?** *(He turns to leave, stops)* In the Ukraine, they ran out of trees, so they manufactured mobile hanging racks. We captured one outside Lvov. It had wheels on, and the maker's name, G. FABEN OF ESSEN. There was a rush of anger, and we brought up hammers to smash the rack, but a counter-barrage drove us into cover. When we returned, the rack was gone. Later, I saw the rack again, not in the Ukraine, but in Galicia, hitched behind one of our trucks. It was going back again, like the plough over Europe. G. FABEN OF ESSEN. *(Pause)* The womb knows no ideology. The womb is innocent. The enemy is ideology. You tell him. He'll listen to you. *(He goes out.* SORGE *walks)*

SORGE.   During the battle for the Pripet Marshes there was a panic in the regiment. Vital positions were abandoned, and the enemy rolled up the whole left flank. It was decided to execute, as an example to the others, every seventh man who fled. I was given the responsibility for this, and I did it by choosing every soldier whose christian name began with K. This yielded more than the number we required, so I excluded those whose christian name ended with Y. I chose these letters randomly from a lexicon. This struck some as arbitrary, but was it any more arbitrary than the falling of the enemy's shells? The struggle we set ourselves is to overcome the randomness of nature, which we accept with pagan resignation, and replace it by the ordering of man, which can be random too, sometimes. How have you survived the fascist occupation?

ILONA.   I have an aura.

SORGE.   Really? Do you mean you have a light round you?

ILONA.   Yes.

SORGE.   I can't see it.

ILONA.   Where is my sister?

SORGE *(sitting).*   Let's talk about photography.

ILONA.   She went to Czernovitz.

SORGE.   For example, the problem of selection.

ILONA.   I couldn't understand why she had gone to Czernovitz. Perhaps she was in love with someone.

SORGE.   It's an art of selection, is it not?

ILONA.   She would travel five thousand miles to be with someone. She crossed frontiers for love the way armies cross them for murder.

SORGE.   So the art is not in the picture but the frame.

ILONA.   I was on the Black Sea and she was in Galicia. And then I got a postcard. This postcard followed me from Dedogatch to Bratislava. What is it about a postcard that it passes through wars with no more than a dog-ear when every ditch is full of people whose faces have been crushed? I felt such affection for this postcard that could slip through wars and politics. But it was readdressed so often I couldn't read what she had said, only the name of this place, Czernovitz. And I thought no more about it, until, without knowing it, we came to Czernovitz. Only it isn't like the postcard any more. Where is she, please? *(Pause)*

SORGE.   I've looked with great interest at the photographs. Technically, they can't be criticized. *(Pause. She concedes)* It's not in the technical area I have reservations. It's in the content. Would you care to discuss this?

ILONA.   Yes.

SORGE.   Because I feel sure you will agree the idea of a neutral art is utterly redundant. Yet these images strive for neutrality. Or, to be more precise, they form a background for your face.

ILONA.   I like my face.

SORGE.   Your face is perfectly all right.

ILONA.   It's more than all right.

SORGE.   That's the matter of—

ILONA.   Oh, come on! *(Pause)*

SORGE.   What do you wish me to say? You tell me and I'll say it.

ILONA.   No, you say it. *(Pause)*

SORGE.   You have a beautiful face. *(Pause)* I merely wondered why you choose to decorate these pictures with it.

ILONA.   I was a fashion model. We wanted some different backgrounds. Of course the clothes aren't up to much—

SORGE.   It costs us half a million soldiers in this war for every hundred miles! *(Pause)* We will find the collaborators and we will punish them. It is a duty and a debt. **Are you aware how perilous your position is?** *(Pause)*

ILONA.   Yes.

SORGE *(sitting, with papers)*.   What is your nationality?

ILONA.   Hungarian.

SORGE.   How old are you?

ILONA.   27.

SORGE.   Where are your papers?

ILONA.   In the handbag of the person who is pretending to be me.

SORGE.   They were stolen?

ILONA.   Yes.

SORGE.   When did this happen?

ILONA.   1943.

SORGE.   Why have you not applied for fresh papers?

IILONA.   We haven't been near Budapest.

SORGE.   You have travelled without documents since 1943?

ILONA.   Yes.

SORGE.   Impossible.

ILONA.   It happened.

SORGE.   How did it happen? *(Pause)* A Hungarian fashion model and a Roumanian Jew wander round Europe casually photographing atrocities. They are still alive after four years. *(Pause)* Go away and think about it. Then come back and tell me how it happened. *(Pause. She gets up)* People say to me—people like Arkov say—where is the honour in the secret police? Be a soldier, cluster round the turret of a T34, kills Germans and grin black-faced from the newsreels! Thrill your sister! Make your mother weep! *(She looks at him)* He must have killed a hundred Germans! Simple, clean and honourable, face to face! But me? An officer of NKVD? I must be evil because I work by stealth! *(He gets up)* What sort argument is that? *(Pause)*

ILONA.   Ludicrous. *(He walks up and down)*

SORGE.   I hate simplicity. The intellectual laziness, the posturing of so-called simple men. They float through the world like icebergs, one tenth of sunlit ice. . . but what about the nine-tenths in the dark? *(He turns)* The contradictions? The counter-arguments? The necessary and the expedient? What about them?

ILONA.   Quite. *(She starts to go)*

SORGE. If, when all the smoke has blown away, and Arkov has gone home to his wife, the old black rats of Europe shake the brick-dust from their fur and creep out into the light, what was it all worth, Arkov's blood? What was it worth? *(Pause)*

ILONA. I think you knew my sister. . .

SORGE. I have stood in doorways in the drizzle, watching a guilty lightbulb throb through dirty curtains, Mayakovsky in one pocket, a Sitka .45 in the other, and hour after hour kept warm from knowing there was a child somewhere whose life would, but for my vigilance, be spoiled like all his ancestors had been spoiled until Comrade Lenin got his fingers round the mad dog's throat. . . . *(Pause)* First, there is rebellion, which is easy, and then comes service, which is hard . . .

ILONA. She said that, didn't she? History is a mad dog, I know that's her . . . *(Pause)*
When the mad dog comes for you
Don't run, you'll only stumble.
Instead, lie down and show your throat,
Some dogs don't bite the humble . . .

SORGE. You have a dirty face.

ILONA. She had clear eyes, eyes which made lying impossible.

SORGE. I can give you soap.

ILONA. And a smell like apples. Not like me. My bad breath is legendary. I think your smell comes from your soul, don't you? You blame the bowel, but really the bowel is only—

SORGE *(tossing a piece of soap)*. Wash yourself.

Pause. The chanting of the soldiers in darkness.

ALL. Party card, party card, Number Twelve million, six hundred and sixteen thousand, four hundred and twenty eight, all your power, all your power, lend us at this hour—*(*MELANKOV *tosses down his party card)* Uncle Joe, Uncle Joe, guarding us wherever we go . . . *(A photograph of* STALIN *is added)*

MELANKOV. The Great Teacher . . .

GASSOV. The Great Leader . . .

NEESKIN. The Great Gardener . . .

ARKOV. The Great Pilot . . . . *(Pause)*

MELANKOV. Matches.

NEESKIN. Oh, God . . . .

MELANKOV. Matches!

NEESKIN. I'm not lighting it . . . !

GASSOV. Who asked you to?

NEESKIN. We could get twenty-five years for this, and twenty-five consecutive—

MELANKOV. Sonia, we are releasing the power of the party. It must be burned, all right?

NEESKIN. Couldn't we just—

MELANKOV. What!

NEESKIN. Rub it, or something . . . .

MELANKOV.   Rub it . . . fucking hell . . . rub it . . . .

ARKOV.   Hurry up . . . *(MELANKOV strikes a match, ignites the papers)* Begin.

GASSOV *(adding something from a small bag).*   Bit of Private Shenko's jerkin, splashed with brain . . .

NEESKIN *(similarly).*   Grease off the wheels of the hospital train . . .

MELANKOV.   Tuft of hair from a murdered cossack . . .

ARKOV.   Body of the lizard we squashed with the half-track . . .

GASSOV.   Letter from a widow in Novgorod . . .

(The rhythm is broken) Sonia . . .

ARKOV/MELANKOV.   **Sonia!**

GASSOV   Letter from a widow in Novgorod . . .

NEESKIN   Nazi padre's model of God . . .

MELANKOV.   Menstrual blood from the typing pool . . .

ARKOV.   Bone splinter from the machine gun school . . .

(Pause) Bone splinter from—

GASSOV.   Oh, fuck! Fuck! *(He recollects)* Tooth of a priest strung up by the river . . .

NEESKIN.   Little bit of the mascot's liver . . .

ARKOV.   The mascot's liver?

NEESKIN   I didn't get it, he did—

GASSOV.   So that's what happened to—

MELANKOV.   Shut up, you're spoiling the atmosphere!

NEESKIN.   You don't think I'd cut up a bloody dog, do you?

MELANKOV.   Look, do you want an atmosphere or don't you?

ARKOV.   I am very cold, can we—

MELANKOV.   It will be fucking cold if you don't concentrate! *(Pause)* Any more interruptions, just 'and over yer relics and fuck off, all right? If you want to meet the dead, respect the dead.

ARKOV.   I'm sorry, she—

MELANKOV.   I didn't eat the dog, all right? Where were we we?

NEESKIN.   Mascot's liver . . .

MELANKOV.   Right. *(He concentrates)* Syringe used in the treatment of syphilis . . .

ARKOV.   Part of a stocking of the adjutant's mistress . . .

GASSOV.   Page of the Bible printed in Lapp . . .

NEESKIN.   Specimen of Field Marshal's crap . . .

ALL.   Party card, Party card, Number Twelve million, six hundred and sixteen thousand, four hundred and twenty eight, all your power, all your power, lend to us at this hour . . .

Pause. The circle of kneeling soldiers hold hands in the dark. A distant rumble of artillery.

MELANKOV.   What's it like to be dead? *(Pause)* Please, is it—*(Pause)* I shoved a cloth in my gob and went down 'ead-first in my sleeping bag, is that what—*(Pause)* It was black an' I was suffocating, then Festoff saw my boots twitching and pulled me out. 'ow was it when I cut your throat? Did you know you were dying and hate it? *(Pause)* If I 'adn't been there, an' you 'adn't been there, it wouldn't 'ave 'appened, would it? But I was there, an' so were you. Now, was that coincidence, or was it gonna 'appen from the moment you was born? From the day you came out bawlin' on the straw, were you goin' to that wood to 'ave your throat cut by a Russian? Or was it all because you silly buggers fell asleep? **Or did you 'ave to fall asleep so I could do it, was it that?**

ARKOV. I don't think this is very—

MELANKOV. **I am goin' barmy trying' to work this out!** *(Pause, then, invoking the dead)* Come on, you cunt, come on . . . *(Pause)* Come on!

The concrete slab on which they have made their offering begins to move. NEESKIN emits a stifled gasp.

GLORIA. Ich habe kein festuchen, nicht . . . *(The slab is pushed back. The head of a BLONDE WOMAN appears. NEESKIN flees in a surge of panic, joined by GASSOV. MELANKOV, overcome, swoons to the ground)* Was ist gedanken, russ? *(ARKOV stares at her, as with an air of extreme exhaustion, she clambers out of the hole and sits with her head in her hands. She is wearing a dirty SS uniform)* Ich habe nicht, was tot . . . *(Pause. ARKOV looks swiftly over his shoulder)*

ARKOV. Throw your uniform away. *(She looks at him)* Get rid of it. *(Pause)* Before they hang you. *(He looks round again)* Quick, get it off! *(She stares, not understanding. ARKOV goes to her, tugs at her tunic to indicate his meaning. With the resignation of the defeated, she starts to unbutton. Thinking she is submitting to her fate, she lies on the ground. ARKOV slowly comprehends)* I don't mean that. *(Pause)* Get up. I don't mean that. *(Pause)* **I hate that.** *(Terrified, thinking to please him, GLORIA loosens her hair)* **Nein! Nein! I don't mean that!** *(Mad with despair, he drags his pistol out of its holster. MELANKOV, revived, sits up, sees it)*

MELANKOV. Oi!

GLORIA hides her face. ARKOV thrusts the barrel of the pistol down his trousers. There is a shot. He sways. GLORIA opens her eyes.

MELANKOV *(in horror)*. **Help! Mick's shot 'is cock off! 'elp!**
GLORIA *(astonished)*. Was ist gesocht . . .
ARKOV. Trust now . . . trust . . .

The Spontaneous Nature of Historical Decisions

A gramophone is playing in the Kremlin. The symphony ends. MME DONKIN claps. STALIN walks.

STALIN. The artist's head is a boiled egg. You do not slice it off. You tap it gently with a spoon . . . *(They look at him)* I have yet to meet an artist who did not benefit from being tapped. They think they live on their own, but they're mistaken, they live among us, and they have to learn they aren't the only birds on the lake. If they want to sing out of tune, by all means let them do so, but to expect us to construct music halls and pay the wages of the orchestra! No, sing in tune or shit in your own nest. *(POSKREBYSHEV claps)*

DONKIN.   I think the section praising you is most—appropriate.

STALIN.   Which section's that?

DONKIN.   The third movement.

STALIN.   Is that in praise of me?

ZDHANOV.   It says so in the notes.

STALIN.   Of course it says so in the notes. It would do, wouldn't it? I don't read notes. When I'm dead he'll say it was a trick to get past the censors. No, they are ruthless, artists, we have a terrible struggle with them. *(He shrugs)* I've mixed feelings about it . . . .

ZDHANOV.   It's better than the sixth.

STALIN.   That was a bottle of piss!

ZDHANOV.   Yes.

STALIN.   He was up the wrong street there.

ZDHANOV.   Yes.

STALIN.   But we tapped his egg, and you see, he has got better!

MME DONKIN.   He nearly committed suicide.

STALIN.   Did he! did he really? Never mind, he didn't, he became a better composer instead! If they cannot resolve the contradictions, they are better off dead, they know that, they do know that, however much women of special sensitivity pander to their souls . . . .

MME DONKIN *(going to place a new record on the gramophone)*. Khachaturian's fugue for strings and bass.

STALIN.   How do they tap their eggs in the West?

ZDHANOV.   They don't. A gang of musical idiots play in one another's rooms.

MME DONKIN.   Khachaturian's fugue for strings and bass . . . .

STALIN.   Are there any American composers?

ZDHANOV.   No.

STALIN.   Do you think socialism would produce some?

ZDHANOV.   That is a very difficult question.

STALIN.   It is a difficult question. What are material origins of culture?

POSKREBYSHEV.   The Commissar for Nationalities is here—

STALIN.   I'm not against him coming in— *(he turns back to ZDHANOV)* No, we must admit, mustn't we, that the individuality of cultures is only partially dependent on differences in economic relations, or how else should we explain, for example, the peculiar rhythms of the Kirghiz dance—which I cannot bear, incidentally—but which you must admit, is at least their own? (LASHENKO *enters*) It is insufficient, I should have thought, to say that tribal patriarchies invariably produce eight beats to the bar, and feudal oligarchies twelve—

MME DONKIN.   Fugue—

ZDHANOV.   Changes in musical form follow the rise of certain classes, which alone explains the stability of primitive music—

MME DONKIN. —for—strings—and—

STALIN. I understand that, of course, but I am sceptical that the introductive of the collective economy to the United States would produce a Shostakovich—

MME DONKIN. —bass—

STALIN *(silencing them with a lifted finger).* Khachaturian. *(They are silent for some bars. He removes the needle from the record.)* I played Khachaturian during the three days of disasters. While the Germans shattered our defences, I lay down on the floor and listened, and he told me you have made mistakes, now you must correct them. That is what the music said. It didn't soothe me. It instructed me. *(He looks at LASHENKO)* What?

LASHENKO. The landlord question in Estonia.

STALIN. There is no question music has a moral content, but how? How was it Khachaturian restored me at the very moment I felt I had betrayed Lenin and the entire people? I was mad with guilt, I saw their ghosts crowding round the room, and yet in three days I was able to emerge and take control, to restore a situation everybody thought was lost—myself included! How is it moral, Zdhanov? I don't understand.

ZDHANOV. There is a theory that certain melodic structures—

STALIN. He knows! He knows everything! Listen to him!

ZDHANOV. Relate in a very material way to stimulate emotional responses—

STALIN. I'm not talking about emotions, I'm talking about morals—

ZDHANOV. I was coming to that—

STALIN. He was coming to it!

ZDHANOV. And that the emotional responses can be placed in fifteen categories, each of which—

STALIN. Shift them to Transcaucasia. *(Pause)*

LASHENKO. Transcaucasia . . .

STALIN. They know about cattle, don't they? Stick them on collective farms.

LASHENKO *(holding a notebook).* There is a small problem of transport . . .

STALIN. **There are always problems of transport, there is a war on!** *(Pause)* Send them in empty ammunition trucks. *(Pause)* If the Red Army can travel in cattle trucks, I'm certain twenty thousand landlords can. *(Pause)* No, there are so many absurd theories being put about in musicology, but of all the arts it is the least susceptible to materialist orthodoxy. I keep an open mind on it. Someone should compose a symphony to cattle trucks. They have reconstructed Europe.

POSKREBYSHEV. Shall I make a note of that?

STALIN. If I have time I should like to write a paper on it.

POSKREBYSHEV. On—

ZDHANOV. I should be fascinated to read it . . .

POSKREBYSHEV *(confused).* On . . . ?

STALIN. You know, there will never be such a movement of peoples again . . . *(POSKREBYSHEV looks at MME DONKIN)* I think sometimes of a stranger on another planet, fixing his single eye to the lens of a powerful telescope, and bringing Europe into view. Imagine the sheer frenzy that will greet his eyes! An ant-heap kicked into activity, every road and track jammed with civilians or armies jostling one another as they pass, some marching East, some fleeing West, some wandering south, some lost, some under orders, some with guards, some unaccompanied, some crooks, some murderers, the killer and the mother of the killed tramping in opposite directions on the same rutted road, his sack of loot jostling her bag of baby clothes, his curse and her groan. Who knows where he will find himself, by what gate a child will be born, or in what ditch an old woman breathe her last? Is it chaos? Or is it a building site? A building site, to the uninitiated, is the essence of chaos, but to the foreman, merely the first stage of the plan. I am the foreman, and Lenin made the plans. Of course, if you are sitting in a puddle with raw, bloody feet, it is hard to appreciate the beauty of the structure. I understand that! I am perfectly human.

ZDHANOV.   No one misses History. Whether he sees its purpose or not.

STALIN.   That's perfectly true. Neither monks nor beautiful women . . . *(Pause)* What has happened to my sex drive, Lena?

MME DONKIN.   How should I know?

STALIN.   You are a bio-chemist, aren't you? *(Pause, She shrugs)*

MME DONKIN.   You don't see enough skirt. *(ZDHANOV laughs)*

STALIN.   I see your skirt . . . . *(He laughs again)* What about you, Poskrebyshev?

POSKREBYSHEV.   I'm all right, thank you.

STALIN.   Lying bastard.

POSKREBYSHEV.   No, I'm not, I—

STALIN.   You rub yourself. I've seen it. *(ZDHANOV laughs)* He does! I've seen it! Up against the furniture like a dog.

MME DONKIN.   There is something about Comrade Poskrebyshev that leads you to think he prefers to be doing it on his own . . .

STALIN *(laughing)*.   You see, she can tell! Poskrebyshev, what an indictment! How can you tell?

MME DONKIN.   His eyes . . .

STALIN.   His eyes! Poskrebyshev, look into my eyes!

MME DONKIN.   No, that won't—

STALIN.   Look into my eyes! *(ZDHANOV laughs. POSKREBYSHEV looks at STALIN)* they are rather watery eyes . . .

MME DONKIN.   You cannot possibly tell. You are not a woman.

ZDHANOV.   Mystification.

MME DONKIN.   Of course it's not.

ZDHANOV.   Obfuscation.

MME DONKIN.   A man cannot look into a man's eyes the way he looks into a woman's—

ZDHANOV.   Feminine obscurantism—

MME DONKIN.   It's true, something happens to the retina—

ZDHANOV.   If he desires her, of course, but—

STALIN.   Poskrebyshev, she says you hate her cunt. *(Pause)*

POSKREBYSHEV.   I can't say I feel very drawn to . . .
STALIN.   Do you? Hate it? *(Pause)*
POSKREBYSHEV.   Yes. *(They all laugh.* ZDHANOV *and* MME
DONKIN *leave)*

Pause then POSKREBYSHEV, *in bitter despair, attacks* STALIN,
hammering him on the chest. They move, absurdly, round the room, until
POSKREBYSHEV, *exhausted, falls into a chair.* STALIN, *unhurt, goes out
and returns with a glass of water.* POSKREBYSHEV *takes it, sips.* STALIN
replaces the needle on the record.

The Indignation of a Mass Murderer

A MAN *seated in a chair, guarded.*

MATRIMOVA.   The concept of Wholefilm in the developing theory of
cinema, by Galina Matrimova. *(Pause. She adjusts her tommy-gun)*
Wholefilm discards the fundamental contradiction of the bourgeois film—
the autonomy of the director. Until now, all film has been warped by the
interpretation of the single eye. The representation of reality has been
incomplete. Wholefilm entails a spectacular and democractic in-
novation—three screens in a dialectical relationship, producing an
artistic experience which maximalizes the audience's grasp of reality and at
the same time offers the prospect of genuine socialist development. The
screens are numbered one, two, and three. They may also be titled
Psychology, History and Possibility.
BUBER.   What 'ave I got to 'ave my picture taken for? I ain't done no
wrong.
MATRIMOVA.   The screen numbered one relates the subjective view of the
event, perceived from the viewpoint of the individual mind. The bourgeois
phase.
BUBER.   **I wanna talk to somebody!**
MATRIMOVA.   Screen number two places the event in the context of its
historical causality. The Marxist phase.
BUBER.   **Please.**
MATRIMOVA.   Screen number three, which is the synthesis, offers the
alternative prospect available given the conditions described in one and
two, and for the first time places responsibility on the audience, which
escapes its passive role and becomes itself the focus of the new realism!
BUBER.   Excuse me, if I 'ave been liberated, what 'ave I got to 'ave my
picture taken for?
MATRIMOVA.   This is the screen based on the proposition 'if'—
BUBER.   **Nobody talks to me!**
MATRIMOVA.   Whereas the first and second screens are based on the

propositions 'how' and 'but' . . . .

ILONA *and* VICTOR *enter, carrying boxes of photographic plates.*

VICTOR.   I tell you it's gone.

ILONA.   You are looking in the wrong box.

VICTOR *(kneeling by a box).*   How can it be the wrong box? This is the final box, look, there is the desecrated crucifix—*(He removes the plates one by one, holding them out to her)* There is the doll on the rusty bayonet—*(she looks cursorily)* The cattle killed by shellfire—

BUBER.   I want to lodge a protest.

VICTOR.   The abandoned ambulance—**where is it, then?**

ILONA.   All right, it's missing.

VICTOR.   They are going to kill us.

ILONA *(looking at a plate).*   That beret really suited me . . .

VICTOR.   Why do you have to lie, and posture like that? When you are as scared as I am, why?

ILONA.   I am not as scared as you are.

VICTOR.   You are! You are!

ILONA.   No. When it comes to being scared, you are in a class of your own.

BUBER.   There are people walking about who've got a lot more explaining to do than I 'ave. I don't see them 'aving their pictures taken—

VICTOR.   Clinging to your dirty little bit of dignity, your dirty little scrap of sex—

ILONA.   You always get abusive when you're frightened, have you noticed that?

VICTOR.   You're as petrified as I am, you haven't got a hope, why don't you admit it—

ILONA.   **Because I'm not going down on my knees yet.** *(She stares at him. Pause)* Where are the lens hoods? *(She goes to the camera.* VICTOR *gets up, sorts through a bag)*

VICTOR.   I said to him, I am an innocent photographer. He said there is no such thing as an innocent photographer, only photographers with varying degrees of guilt. What does that mean? It's a death sentence. *(He screws the lens hood on)*

BUBER.   What am I supposed to do, smile? I 'aven't got my teeth in—

VICTOR *(as* ILONA *focuses).*   I can't follow the arguments. With the Nazis it was easy, either they liked you or they didn't, and if they didn't, they smashed your jaw, but these

ILONA.   You are getting positively sentimental—

VICTOR.   Everything is argument, and I can't follow arguments. If I could follow arguments, I wouldn't be photographer.

ILONA.   Don't be afraid of the argument. It's just their way of saying if they like you. Just look in their eyes . . . . *(she adjusts the tripod)*

VICTOR.   I can't. I've never looked anyone in the eyes.

ILONA.   Don't despise the eyes,
They don't tell lies, the eyes,
When the pupil shrinks to nothing
It's the bullet or a fucking,

Be wise, forget the words
And watch the eyes . . .
BUBER. That's very good, that's very fucking true that is . . .
ILONA. He likes it.
BUBER. I fucking do . . .
VICTOR *(getting out the drape)*. I believe we have no sensitity in our souls at all, and we are paying for it . . .
ILONA. Oh, dear . . .
VICTOR. I believe we have systematically trodden down our feelings until we no longer know the difference between casualness and cruelty . . . I think I would rather not survive than survive the way we do . . .
ILONA. Rubbish . . .
VICTOR. I think we are going to die and we deserve it!

He turns away from the camera in despair. ILONA *goes to him.*

ILONA. Victor, you've got the sick dog's eyes . . .
VICTOR. Yes . . .
ILONA. The eyes of old men who have sunk down and can't get up again . . . the eyes we've seen on every road in Europe . . . the eyes that beckon rifle butts . . .
VICTOR. I know . . .
ILONA. Victor . . . don't be the left-hand corner of an atrocity. *(*SORGE *enters briskly)*
SORGE. Good morning—
BUBER *(jumping to his feet)*. Everyone did business with the Germans, I wasn't the only one, I made it perfectly clear I would prefer to manufacture for the civilian market, I submitted memoranda on twelve separate occasions saying my factory was not competent to supply synthetic rubber for military purposes—
SORGE. Is it light enough in here? I'm afraid we are rather short of equipment. . .
BUBER. Don't take my word for it, ask my foreman, ask Harry Wilkoska, 'e saw the memoranda, ask 'im—
ILONA *(trying to focus)*. He keeps moving . . .
SORGE. Ask him to retain his seat . . .
BUBER. Far from being a collaborator, I supplied inferior equipment—
MATRIMOVA. Sit down—
BUBER. I initiated a policy of sabotage, not one of the tyres supplied by me was in usable condition, ask Harry Wilkoska—
MATRIMOVA. Sit down—
BUBER. I will sit down—*(He sits)* Why isn't 'e 'ere, if I am, why isn't Harry Wilkoska—
ILONA. Can we bring that light in just a—*(*VICTOR *moves the flood)*
BUBER. —all the products coming out of my factory were substandard— always 'ave been for that matter—
SORGE. Tell him to shut up.
BUBER. Ask anybody, ask Stefan Pillowitz, 'e knows my tyres caused innumerable accidents, so far from—

MATRIMOVA.   Be quiet.

BUBER.   So far from 'elping the Nazi war effort, I made a significant contribution to their defeat, all right, take the fucking thing—*(ILONA presses the shutter)*

MATRIMOVA.   Next! *(She shoves him out)*

SORGE.   I hope the photographs have been returned to you in proper order?

ILONA.   Yes.

VICTOR.   No. *(SORGE looks at them)*

SORGE.   Are you complaining that some damage has been done—

VICTOR.   Yes.

ILONA.   No. *(Pause)* I never had a sister. I don't know why I said I had a sister. I am an only child.

SORGE.   Yes. It's obvious you are an only child. Me too. *(MATRIMOVA hurries in another MAN)*

TOSHACK.   I cannot see any excuse for the arrests of officials of the Peasants' Party, this is an outrage and I refuse to have my photograph taken!

SORGE.   I think we both believe the world belongs to us, which is untrue, of course . . .

TOSHACK.   The policy of the Peasant's Party with regard to the Nazi occupation was not one of collaboration but Negative Accommodation, as laid down by the party congress of 17th August, 1943. This was defined as resistance in principle but accommodation in practice, **I will not sit down,** there's no truth whatsoever in the calumny that we supplied the names of communists to the Gestapo **if I sit down I am admitting guilt**—

SORGE.   Then you have your photograph taken standing up. *(As ILONA adjusts the camera)* They say the single child is not happy. I think I was happy. Perhaps I might have been happier with a sister, how can I ever know? How happy were you with your sister?

ILONA.   I haven't got one. *(Pause. SORGE looks at her, then turns to MATRIMOVA)*

SORGE.   Take the chair away. Everyone is to be photographed standing up. *(He looks at TOSHACK)* You see, you make everything worse for everybody. *(ILONA presses the shutter. MATRIMOVA hurries TOSHACK out)*

ILONA.   When this is done, is it all right if we go? *(Pause)*

SORGE.   Go?

ILONA.   Yes.

SORGE.   Go where? *(She shrugs)* You see, I don't think people will be just going—any more. That is archaic. That is very pre-war, like Cook's tours of the Danube Principalities. Like beggars, and caviar. Just going. Just coming. What does 'can I go' mean? It means 'can I avoid', doesn't it? I think we should say, rather, 'Can I serve?' *(They look at one another)*

ILONA.   That's what I meant . . .

MATRIMOVA *enters with the German SS woman,* GLORIA.

SORGE.   Once there was a necessity for self, for being **me**, for being the opposite of **you**, and the terror of **them**, for wearing yellow trousers and baring your arse on the top of the bus. When the world makes men dead-eyed with servility, and girls weep on the table tops of clubs, **me** is something to get hold of. In the scream of angry night-life, the dirty cocktail of poverty and exotic fucks, yes, you need **me** badly. But the war's killed that. We are all the same now, we all wear the same costume of dirty European mud. No me now. Strip the armour off the tanks, get history in our hot little fingers . . . plasticine . . . plasticine . . . *(Pause. MATRIMOVA applauds)* Galina likes a speech . . . . *(He turns to go, stops)* the unit photographer trod on a mine. Would you do the photographs until he is replaced?

ILONA.   Yes . . . *(SORGE smiles, goes out)*

MATRIMOVA.   When I hear Sorge, I think I will go mad because art fails so much! It settles for so little! There is no point in it, no point at all, unless it is the entire truth! **How can you get the entire truth?** I shall go mad! *(ILONA slides in a new negative plate)*

VICTOR.   They are using us. And killing us later.

ILONA.   Victor, somewhere in the rubble of Europe is a silver-framed photograph of me sitting on Heydrich's lap . . .

VICTOR *(horrified)*.   Will you shut up . . . ?

ILONA.   The Spanish fascists with the female circumcisions in their caps . . . the Italian bomb aimer who wore mascara . . .

VICTOR *(hurrying to the flood)*.   This could do with a reflector, couldn't it?

ILONA.   The Greek police chief with initialled underwear . . .

VICTOR.   What about a reflector in this!

ILONA.   The Captain of the Papal Order of White Cavalry who made me swallow piss . . . .

VICTOR.   Ilona . . . *(He turns away, shaking his head)*

ILONA *(smiles at MATRIMOVA)*.   The wallets of Europe are stuffed with pictures of my face . . . heavily powdered to conceal the bruises I got for being unsatisfactory in bed.

GLORIA *(to ILONA)*.   Do you speak German?

VICTOR.   I am going to New York. I am going to sit in a bar. That's all. Sit in a bar in New York.

GLORIA.   I want to tell you who I killed and who I didn't.

VICTOR.   For the rest of my life. Just sit in a bar in New York.

GLORIA.   Listen, will you?

GLORIA.   I took part in the massacre at Gorshin.

ILONA.   Which Gorshin?

GLORIA.   On the Dneiper. I shot half a dozen children in the neck.

ILONA.   Keep still, please.

GLORIA.   I beat a woman to death in Monasterzhiska.

ILONA.   That's lovely . . . . *(She presses the shutter)*

GLORIA.   I assisted at the gassing of the gypsies at Hyak.

ILONA *(removing the plate)*.   Why are you telling me this?

GLORIA.   Two hundred and forty-seven individuals.

ILONA *(turning away).*   All right, she can go. *(*MATRIMOVA *goes to push her out)*

GLORIA.   But not the woman in the overcoat. *(Pause)*

ILONA.   What woman?

GLORIA.   He says the woman in the overcoat. I did not touch the woman in the overcoat.

MATRIMOVA.   I think we need to move a little quicker—

GLORIA.   My name is Gloria Hertfeldz, Jugenfrau SS. I did not touch the woman in the overcoat. *(*MATRIMOVA *escorts her out)*

VICTOR.   Got to get out, Ilona. Before they shut the garden gates on us.

ILONA *(absently).*   Yes . . .

VICTOR.   **I don't ask a lot from life.** *(She looks at him)*

ILONA.   Don't you?

VICTOR.   To be left alone . . .

ILONA.   You don't think that's a lot! He say that's not a lot to ask from life!

VICTOR.   **It's not!** *(He strides, desperately, stops)* You've changed.

ILONA.   Have I?

VICTOR.   You know you have.

ILONA.   No, I don't know, how have I?

VICTOR.   It's obvious.

ILONA.   What's obvious about it? What? If it's obvious why don't you tell me?

PROKASH *(propelled into the room).*   Michael Korvash says I spoke to the Germans! So I spoke to the Germans! Didn't Michael Korvash speak to the Germans? They were living in my house for four years, what was I supposed to do, have my tongue out?

VICTOR.   You are in love.

She stares at him. Blackout.

She Did Not Die for Love, But for Its Impossibility

A field at night. The sound of shovels.

GASSOV.   I have a theory about God. Do you want to hear it? *(There is no reply)* I'm not claiming it's original. Anyone who claims to be original's a fool. How do you ever know if you're original? All you're saying is you've never heard it said before. Somebody has almost certainly thought your thought but hasn't had the vanity to express it. So I don't say that. I only say I have a theory. *(Pause)* According to my theory God is neither good nor bad. He is stupid. Once you accept that He is stupid, all questions of belief fall into place. For example, the question, does He exist or not, becomes irrelevant, like the question or responsibility. We say of Him, as we say of an insane murderer, He is responsible for the crime of which He is accused, but not guilty of it. God is responsible for the world, but not guilty of it. This is a God you could get very fond of. Now, I don't say He was always stupid. That is a theological question. He was driven stupid, in

all probability, by the spectacle of His works. *(Pause)* Butt in if you want
to . . . .

SORGE *(entering)*. Why do you talk religion so incessantly? All this
metaphysics, but the hole is not getting any deeper.

MELANKOV. 'e started it.

GASSOV. I never stopped digging, did I? I can think and dig.

MELANKOV. You call that thinking? That is the wanderin' of an
unhinged mind.

SORGE. All pain leads to metaphysics. It's a problem for the party. I could
not help noticing, as we advanced, how our soldiers grew in superstition in
direct ratio to the numbers of the dead.

GASSOV. Oh?

SORGE. But the opposite should be the case! The greater the pain, the
greater the demand for reason. Didn't I love her enough? Why should they
hang her? Please leave me.

GASSOV *(shouldering his shovel)*. Give us your pistol.

SORGE. My pistol? Why? *(Pause)* Oh! *(He laughs)* He thinks—I say I
loved her and he thinks—

GASSOV. I know it's silly but—

SORGE *(sarcastically)*. **Just in case.**

Pause, then SORGE *removes his holster and gives it to* GASSOV. *The*
SOLDIERS *go out.* SORGE *stands by* HANNELA'S *body.*

SORGE. I am not unforgiving. I forgive everything. Accusing, forgiving,
under the junk of wasted wars the words lie rotting **love is not to do with
truth** if it was there would be none I am not shouting it is you who shouts
yes you you shout because you don't possess the arguments it is a matter of
correctness not of volume if you cannot solve the contradiction you will
become not the maker nor the collaborator in the making of your time but
the mud in which the feet of passing armies left their print your flesh is oh
your flesh is do not look at me with pity I hate that no one to pity me your
arrogant curled lip in wilful incomprehension goes even in death goes
(He sees a figure in the gloom) Yes? (TREMBLAYEV *looks at him. Pause*)
You shouldn't wander in uncleared fields, they're full of unexploded
things. Did you know the champagne in the cellar was booby-trapped?

TREMBLAYEV. I think you must be stopped.

SORGE. Stopped? Don't tell me you have climbed over all this desolation
just to tell me I have to be stopped. Stopped from what?

TREMBLAYEV. I believe you are exercizing a personal hegemony which
endangers the safety of the 12th Motorized Brigade. While the party has
reason to be grateful to you you must know that no one is indispensable—

SORGE *(shaking his head)*. No—

TREMBLAYEV. That it is the duty of every one of us to—

SORGE. No—

TREMBLAYEV. Be vigilant in the interests of—

SORGE. What is it? *(Pause)* Nadia? *(Pause)*

TREMBLAYEV. It is impossible to serve the party and to indulge in personal relationships.

SORGE. I am not aware of any injunction which forbids—

TREMBLAYEV. That isn't the point. There is no injunction against gardening either, but if the regimental political officer spent the entire day planting onions, there would be cause for—

SORGE. Nadia—

TREMBLAYEV. Do not use my christian name—

SORGE. Comrade Tremblayev, what is your evidence for this? *(Pause)*

TREMBLAYEV. I'm not blind . . .

SORGE. On the contrary, I think you see things no one else can—

TREMBLAYEV. Do not touch me—

SORGE. I wasn't going to touch you—

TREMBLAYEV. I must tell you I have escaped from you—

SORGE. I am delighted—

TREMBLAYEV. Which she did not. *(Pause)*

SORGE. What are you saying?

TREMBLAYEV. Secret burial is—

SORGE. What are you saying—

TREMBLAYEV. Against the regulations—

SORGE. No, you said—

TREMBLAYEV. The Germans did not hang her. *(Pause)* Did they?

SORGE. I have arrested the SS officer responsibile for her murder—

TREMBLAYEV. Sorge, it is a lie—

SORGE. **I cannot allow the discipline of the unit to be undermined like this. I am charging you.**

TREMBLAYEV. I am simply telling you the truth—

SORGE. Simply telling me the truth! The plea of counter-revolution through the ages, the whine of a spurious morality drawn like a veil over sinister intentions! When I hear someone say I am simply telling the truth I know I am in the presence of the enemy. Surrender your pistol.

TREMBLAYEV. No, I won't do that.

SORGE. Very well, I—*(He reaches for his holster. It is empty)* **Gassov is in this with you!**

TREMBLAYEV. In what?

SORGE. **This!**

TREMBLAYEV. What?

SORGE. Conspiracy!

TREMBLAYEV. There is no conspiracy, I only—

SORGE. **No conspiracy, where is my pistol, then?** *(There is a crack of a rifle offstage.* SORGE *collapses to his knees)* All right, shoot me! Shoot me!

GASSOV. Sorge! Sorge!

SORGE *(turning to him)*. **Traitor!**

GASSOV. Wha'—Wha's he—

SORGE. What's the matter, Gassov, **got no guts?** You point it there and pull the trigger!

GASSOV. Melankov's shot the photographer! *(Pause)*

SORGE.   Which photographer?

MELANKOV *(rushing on with his rifle).* **I 'ate shooting people! I 'ate shooting people!**

SORGE *(scrambling to his feet, grabbing* MELANKOV*)* **Which photographer! Which photographer!**

MELANKOV.   Take the fuckin' rifle!

SORGE.   **The woman or the man!**

GASSOV.   The man. *(*SORGE *releases* MELANKOV, *who sobs violently)*

MELANKOV *(to* GASSOV*).*   I shouted three times, you 'eard me, three times, didn't I—

SORGE *(in full possession of himself).*   Go and inspect the body. Ascertain if he is dead and—

MELANKOV.   **Three times I said**—

SORGE.   **Control yourself!** *(Pause)* Take the body to the hospital and write it in the book.

MELANKOV.   Can't write.

SORGE.   Very well. Wake up a stenographer. Go on. *(*MELANKOV *slouches away)* And take your rifle. *(He returns, pick it up)* Good. *(Pause)* Good.

A Degree of Suffering Is Required

ILONA, *by a bowl of water.*

MATRIMOVA.   I think you wash your hair too much.

ILONA.   No, if anything, I don't do it enough.

MATRIMOVA.   And your back . . . . *(she places her hands on* ILONA'S *back)*

ILONA.   Spotty as ever . . . .

MATRIMOVA.   He is coming tonight, and your hair will be wet for his fingers to fasten on. And the next day, you will go about in his jeep, and he will plunder all the shops for you . . . .

ILONA.   Yes . . .

MATRIMOVA.   What a beautiful couple!

ILONA.   I have been the half of so many beautiful couples. Plundering this way, and plundering that . . .

MATRIMOVA.   When the war is over, I will make a film, and you will be in it, you will be—everything! What was, what is, what should have been! *(She jumps up)* He's coming! *(She listens)* The heeltap of the virile boot . . . . *(Pause)* And stops . . .

ILONA.   Why?

MATRIMOVA.   Removes his boots . . .

ILONA.   Why?

MATRIMOVA.   Comes to your door in socks . . . . and says . . . *(she looks up, affectedly)* Listen to the rain . . . . *(she hurries out. SORGE enters. He looks at her)*

SORGE.   Listen to the rain, churning up the mud and beckoning the corpses . . . up they come . . . elbows and knees . . . labouring through fields and gardens . . . by morning there will be a show of clotted heads like crocuses . . . *(Pause)* What do you know about Victor Barbu?

ILONA.   He is a left-handed photographer from Ploiesti. He has no special talent, but he's good at judging exposures. He has an eye for light, but none for composition. He drives the Ford. He is clever with engines. I say engines, I mean the plugs. Not the plugs, exactly, the gaps. He once saved fifteen litres of petrol by adjusting the gaps. I never saw him touch a woman. Nor a man either. He gets bad headaches, but aspirin make him sick. *(Pause)* That is all I know of Victor Barbu.

SORGE.   He was shot at eleven fifty-three last night, slipping through the compound fence with two crates of photographs. He ignored three warnings. I'm afraid some of the negatives are broken. *(Pause)*

ILONA.   Well, of course.

SORGE.   It is very hard to shoot accurately in the dark.

ILONA.   It was most inconsiderate of him. I think if someone is going to get shot, they ought to present a proper target.

SORGE.   I think you are deeply hurt.

ILONA.   Victor is dead because he wanted to be dead. New York was just— a metaphor.

SORGE.   You are—deeply shocked and so you—

ILONA.   I have seen a lot of corpses—

SORGE.   But this one you knew!

ILONA.   Superficially—

SORGE.   Three years and you say—

ILONA.   Superficially.

SORGE.   Night after night, beneath the stars, mile after mile on rutted roads . . . .

ILONA.   There are tears in your eyes! I've always said, if you don't cry someone else will always do it for you—*(he grabs her by the shoulders)* Why do you want me to cry! To reassure you all the old emotions are still knocking around? To show you women are still women—*(he strikes her. Pause)*

When the man with blood all down his coat
Puts his fingers round your throat,
It's not the prelude to your dying,
You're only the audience for a little manly crying . . .

SORGE *(turning away)*.   I have to make love to you.

ILONA.   What, now?

SORGE.   You have no idea how I'm suffering—

ILONA.   You are—

SORGE.   Yes, terribly suffering—

ILONA.   Yes—

SORGE.   You must be serious—

ILONA. Yes—

SORGE. And warm—

ILONA. Whatever you say—

SORGE. And giving—

ILONA. You are hurting me—

SORGE. **Must! Must!** *(He pulls away from her)* When I set eyes on you . . . the mud splashed on your calves and your crushed shoes I felt—how pure she is . . . through all this clamour she walks untouched . . . .

ILONA. What do you want me to—

SORGE. Shh . . . shh . . .

ILONA. I am perfectly happy to be your—

SORGE *(waving a hand)*. Shh . . . . *(Pause)* I felt . . . she is unspoiled by History . . . . *(Pause)* I want to you **want** to be my mistress . . . . *(Pause)*

ILONA. Well, I do. *(Pause)*

SORGE. No, you see, there is this acquiescence in you which—

ILONA. Yes, I'm sorry, it's a thing I picked up—

SORGE. Not to acquiesce, but to will, and therefore—to suffer . . .

ILONA. Yes . . .

SORGE. For wanting . . . . *(Pause)*

ILONA. I do suffer.

SORGE. I expect so much from love.

ILONA. Me, too.

SORGE. **You agree so much it makes me suspicious.**

ILONA. It's a habit, it's, I—real feelings become—after so much—become —impossible to—

SORGE. Perhaps you should resist me—

ILONA. Perhaps I should, yes—

SORGE. **Resist me, then!**

ILONA. Anything that has substance will be snapped, and anything that hasn't, can't be. She had substance, didn't she. So much substance I really hated her—

SORGE. I insist you are yourself—

ILONA. I am trying—

SORGE. No, you are hiding, you are hiding something, no one can be so—

ILONA. I am, I am myself—

SORGE. Let me make some mark on you, what are you, a saint! *(He kisses her violently, painfully. Pause)*

ILONA. I think she killed herself. She did. She killed herself to get away from you.

Pause. A MAN *in an overcoat enters. He is holding Sorge's boots.*

MAN IN OVERCOAT. I saw your boots! Outside, together. The boots. And I thought, Oh God, he is naked, but. So I came in. You are not naked. Sometimes to catch the lovers naked fills me with. So thank goodness. *(He holds out the boots.* TREMBLAYEV *enters.)*

TREMBLAYEV. You are under arrest.

SORGE. On what charge?

TREMBLAYEV. The charge follows the investigation. You know that very well.

SORGE.   I shall extract the highest penalty for this! *(The* MAN IN OVERCOAT *strikes him.* SORGE *is silent.)*

MAN IN OVERCOAT.   I hate shouting. He doesn't have to shout to make a point, does he?

SORGE.   Comrade Tremblayev is an officer of the NKVD, she has every right to investigate what is probably a routine matter—*(to* ILONA) I love you, do you love me—there will be a cross-examination and I—do you love me?

ILONA *does not reply.* THE MAN IN OVERCOAT *indicates to* SORGE. *They leave.*

TREMBLAYEV.   Your sister is buried by the anti-aircraft trench . . .

She goes out. ILONA *is alone.*

TREMBLAYEV.   Your sister is buried by the anti-aircraft trench . . . *(she goes out.* ILONA *is alone)*

MATRIMOVA *(rushing in).*   Sorge has been arrested! They've gone off with Sorge!

ILONA.   Yes . . .

MATRIMOVA.   Sorge! Why Sorge?

ILONA.   **It is very difficult to wash your hair round here!**

MATRIMOVA.   He must have done wrong, mustn't he? Mustn't he? It's impossible, but why would they arrest him otherwise? He's arrested, therefore he's done wrong. It's unbelievable! *(She is surging to and fro)* I don't understand how you—I mean, if the impossible is true, where does that leave—how does an artist cope with that? If the absolutely true is absolutely false, how do you—*(Pause)* It calls for a fourth screen! A Fourth Screen which says—notwithstanding all that has been registered on screens one to three—there is always the possibility that—*(she holds her head, agonized)* I shall never make a film.

ILONA.   Oh, don't say that—

MATRIMOVA.   No, never make one. *(She stares at* ILONA) Don't you even care about the truth?

ILONA.   No. *(Pause)*

MATRIMOVA.   Please, may I kiss you before you go?

ILONA.   If you want to. *(She inclines a cheek)*

MATRIMOVA.   No, your feet . . . . *(She kisses* ILONA'S *feet)* I think you are very near to God . . . .

ILONA.   Go? *(Pause)* Go where?

MATRIMOVA.   Everyone will miss you.

ILONA.   **Go where.**

MATRIMOVA *shakes out a tape-measure and holds it against* ILONA'S *back, letting the end fall to the floor. She Reads it.*

MATRIMOVA.   Yes! You are under five feet six!

History Encounters its Antithesis

A room with floodlamps. ILONA *is standing by a tripod and camera.*

McGROOT. There were three hundred and forty-eight photographers, and all of 'em were under five feet six. Which one had the unmarked grave? *(*ILONA *drops a film plate)*

ILONA. Shit.

McGROOT. Correct. The one who shot the emperor. Said one lens to the other, have ye seen any guid subjects lately? An' the furst lens says, A seen a weddin', A seen a christenin', A seen a funeral, an' A seen a donkey fuckin' a woman. Tha's funny, says the other lens, A seen two people tellin' lies in a church, A seen a baby dipped in water, A geezer dropped doon a hole an' a woman carryin' a donkey on her back, where were yoo? *(*STALIN *enters,* POSKREBYSHEV *at his elbow. Long pause)*

POSKREBYSHEV. We came up with three hundred and forty-eight photographers under five feet six. This is Ilona Ferenczy.

ILONA. Good morning, General Secretary. *(Pause. He looks at her painfully and long)*

STALIN. How did her talent assert itself above the other three hundred and forty-seven, I ask myself . . .

POSKREBYSHEV. There was a short list of ten. Four had relatives serving sentences, three had visited America, and two were party members. The other committed suicide.

ILONA. I was in luck. He cut his throat with a sunlight filter. *(Pause.* STALIN *stares at her)*

STALIN. You are to photograph me as I am.

ILONA. Yes.

STALIN. Yes, she says . . . !

McGROOT. She says yes. She cud say maybe, but she says yes! Ye canna blame her, maybe's hanging off a meathook and noo died of electric shocks. I tease, I tease!

STALIN. It is very difficult to photograph Stalin as he is. Who is Stalin? One day he was in the film, and the next they rubbed him off.

ILONA. I—

STALIN. It is fraught with risks.

ILONA. Is it? Isn't it a face like any other? *(*POSKREBYSHEV *coughs in alarm)*

McGROOT. Yoo do the coughin', A'll do the shittin', **who said tha'**? *(He pretends to hold his bowels)* Pass the sugar, how's ye mother, gotta ticket for the Celtic? Come agin? *(He cups his ear towards* ILONA*)*

STALIN. It is possible I do not actually know my face, and being presented with it, I may become enraged. Have you considered that?

ILONA. No.

STALIN. My skin, for example. Always, they remove the pocks.

ILONA. I shan't do that. Every pock will be included.

McGROOT. Noo pock filters!

STALIN.   Why are you so anxious to be agreeable?

McGROOT.   Yes, why are ye so anxious to be agreeable, cud it be that this is Joseph fuckin' Stalin, **doon't tell me!**

STALIN.   Has she heard that dictators like to be agreed with?

ILONA.   I think, when it comes to portraits, you—

STALIN.   I do not like to be agreed with. I like the last word. *(Pause)*

ILONA.   Yes.

STALIN.   Another problem is my shyness.

ILONA.   Yes.

STALIN.   I despise flamboyance. I despise eccentricity.

ILONA.   I can tell.

STALIN.   Elegance. Rhetoric. The cultivated gesture. How can you trust the man who thinks himself attractive?

ILONA.   Impossible.

STALIN.   Trotsky had a cult of personality if anybody did. If I stood on a poor man's toe I would apologize. The handsome man, when he stands on your toe, he expects you to apologize! Since Stalin, there is no smallpox any more. All the children will have lovely skin, but I ask myself if that is necessarily an advantage? How many will be warped by their good looks? *(She looks at him)*

ILONA.   I'll take the photographs, and you do the talking—

STALIN.   I must go for a piss. *(POSKREBYSHEV helps him up. They go out)*

McGROOT.   The great man says to his bladder, yoo are a treacherous bastard, yoo are, yoo—

ILONA *drops a glass plate. He looks at her. She puts her hands to her head.*

ILONA.   I'm losing it . . . . . I'm losing it . . . . *(STALIN returns)*

STALIN.   I had a request from Karsh of Ottawa. He wanted to put me in his album. He wanted me between King George and a horse-faced English actress.

ILONA *(fiddling with the camera).*   Karsh of Ottawa . . . ?

STALIN.   Does it not show a profound ignorance of art to think you could put Stalin next to George VI? It is not a face I have here, it is a history. *(She photographs him, emerges from the hood)*

ILONA.   But at the same time you are very ordinary!

McGROOT *(horrified).*   So the mouse said to the elephant, no, I didn't borrow the saucepan, the squirrel did! What's the weather like in Durban?

ILONA *(undeterred).*   I wouldn't look at you twice in the street. I can say that because you are not vain. *(She looks at him, lining up the camera)* For example, I know you are not happy in that tunic. *(She focuses)* The epaulettes and so on. You don't spend half the morning at the mirror—stay like that—*(She slides across the plate)* thinking, Joseph—It is Joseph, isn't it—I will have the white suit, no I won't, I'll have the black—that's not your way at all—*(again she drops a plate)* Fuck. *(A long silence)*

STALIN.   I think she is afraid of me.

McGROOT.   Afraid of yoo! Noo, it's no possible, who cud be frightened of
a nice ol' man like yoo? A cud put ma head on his chest an' say, gi' us a
cuddle, uncle! *(He insinuates himself onto STALIN)*

STALIN.   I enjoy frightening people. Isn't it odd that a man of my stature
should enjoy frightening little girls from Budapest? Really, Poskrebyshev,
it's despicable, isn't it?

POSKREBYSHEV.   Well, I suppose it—

STALIN.   It is! It is!

McGROOT.   It fuckin' is—

ILONA *(reviving)*.   There's nothing wrong with fear. I've been frightened
all my life. It's panic you have to worry about. *(He looks at her)* Stay like
that. *(She sets up)*

STALIN.   Give me a kiss. *(Pause)* Give me a kiss. *(Pause, then she goes to
him, takes his hand and kisses it, then returns to the tripod)* The idea of
intimacy with Stalin is absurd. It is absurd, even to Stalin . . . . *(Pause)*
What does she think I have in my trousers, a brick!

McGROOT.   Wha'd ye think he's got in his trousers, a brick! There was a
mon goin' aboot wi' a brick in his trousers, an' a cock on his head—

STALIN.   Must piss.

McGROOT.   Okay, that's all, anyway.

STALIN *and* POSKREBYSHEV *go out.*

ILONA *(shutting her eyes to concentrate)*.   Don't be clever, don't be shy,
don't be vulgar, don't be wise, don't be fruity, don't be arid, don't be
honest, don't tell lies—

POSKREBYSHEV *returns.*

POSKREBYSHEV.   He likes you. *(Pause.* STALIN *returns)*

STALIN.   I have a chill on my bladder. Against the little plots of nature,
even Stalin is not proof.

ILONA *(to POSKREBYSHEV)*.   Would you remove his cap? Otherwise,
we shall be honouring the cap. *(*POSKREBYSHEV *looks to STALIN)* It's
a perfectly nice cap, but— *(*STALIN *stares at her)* There has to be a
Stalin without the cap. *(Pause. He suddenly flings it to the floor)* Yes! *(She
focuses)* That's just—Yes! *(She is under the drape)*

STALIN.   I understand you are under sentence of death. *(Long pause. She
slides it across. Then she emerges)* Lieutenant Sorge had evidence that you
posed on a mass murderer's lap. *(Pause)*

ILONA.   Oh?

STALIN.   For some reason the lieutenant neglected to act on the evidence.
He continually filed your case to the back.

McGROOT.   They do that, doon't they, it's called desire. How do ye knoo
when a man loves you? He puts flowers on yer grave. **A've seen it happen.**

STALIN.   Why, I wonder? *(Pause)*

ILONA.   You should ask him. Now, how about a profile—

STALIN.   I don't think we can do that, can we Poskrebyshev?

ILONA.   Or three-quarters, turned to—*(Pause, she is drained)* Why?

STALIN.   We can't, can we, Poskrebyshev?

POSKREBYSHEV.   No, we can't . . . .

ILONA.   Can't ask him . . . . why . . . . *(STALIN looks at her, then goes to get up)* **Don't get up I haven't finished yet.**

McGROOT *(desperately)*.   There was a parrot locked in a museum, and the mouse said to the prime minister, wha'd yer want in yer sandwich, Michael, can ye follow this, A'm fucked if A can . . . . .

ILONA.   Save him, please. *(Pause)* Save him. *(He looks at her a long time. ILONA sees her mistake, struggles)* No, that was silly, where were we? We were doing—

POSKREBYSHEV.   Thank you, the session is over—

ILONA.   Can't be over, only done four plates, and broke two, so—

POSKREBYSHEV.   Four is all that is required—

ILONA.   I think with Joseph the profile will be most rewarding and we—

POSKREBYSHEV *(helping STALIN up)*.   Good day.

ILONA *(closing her eyes)*.   Am I going to die?

STALIN *(turning)*.   Dying? Who said anything about dying? *(He turns to POSKREBYSHEV)* Have you been frightening Miss—*(he loses the name)* with tales of dying? I cannot go for a piss without Poskrebyshev taking advantage of my absence to throw his weight about. What are you, a sexual pervert? *(He turns to ILONA. He extends his arms. She falls into them)* There . . . there . . . .

ILONA.   Are we safe . . ..

STALIN.   There . . . .

McGROOT.   **Oh, Christ, it kills all comedy, I have no jokes for it.** *(STALIN releases her. McGROOT staggers)* The crocodile says, noo, the alligator, the alligator it was, the alligator says—*(STALIN and POSKREBYSHEV leave)* Listen to th' alligator! *(The light dims gradually. Men enter and carry away the equipment)* The alligator says . . . . . Says . . . . **Listen to the alligator, will ya . . . ?**

The light shrinks.